Black and Deaf in America

Are We That Different

Ernest Hairston
&
Linwood Smith

© 1983 by Ernest Hairston and Linwood Smith

Cover design by Eugene Orr

T.J. PUBLISHERS, INC.
817 Silver Spring Avenue, 206
Silver Spring, Maryland 20910

Printed in the United States of America. All rights reserved.
ISBN #0-932666-18-3   softbound
Library of Congress Catalog No.: 83-050070

First Printing June, 1984
Second Printing July, 1998
Third Printing February, 2002

*To Darlene, Tisha, Mayumi, and all
other children.*

Contents

Acknowledgements

We wish to convey our thanks to the many people who helped make this book possible. In particular, we would like to express our appreciation to Dr. Doris L. Dickens, Director of the Mental Health Program for the Deaf, St. Elizabeths Hospital, Washington, D.C., and Dr. Malcolm J. Norwood, Chief of the Captioned Films and Media Application Branch of Special Education Programs, U.S. Department of Education, for their encouragement and patience.

We are also indebted to the following people who consented to be interviewed for our chapter, *Common Bonds and Stepping Stones:* Shirley Allen, Katie Brown, Mary Cheese, Andrew Foster, Jeremiah Germany, James Magness, Carolyn McCaskill, Chuck Williams, Albert Rhodes, and Albert Couthen.

The photographic collections which enliven this book were generously shared by the Childress, Luckey, Robinson, and Shorter families; and by Black Deaf Advocates; Deafpride, Incorporated; and the National Association of the Deaf.

A special thanks goes to Lottie Crook who gave us constructive criticism and the push needed to accomplish our task and to Mencie M. Yaquil-Hairston for invaluable editorial assistance.

Family members and relatives also deserve our gratitude for their understanding, tolerance, and encouragement.

Foreword

Being both Black and deaf is in many ways a "double whammy" because of society's abrogation of each of these two minorities. When the conditions of Blackness and deafness are combined in one person, the individual effects of prejudice, discrimination, and negative self-image are compounded exponentially. For example, a disproportionate percent of Black deaf youth are educated in urban schools where the programs are often unbelievably bad. In many of these schools, the Black child is mainstreamed with few, if any, supportive services, or else he is placed in classes with retarded children or those having other disabilities totally unrelated to his own. The results are devastating.

The ramifications of deafness, the lack of sufficient Black role models, and the overall racial situation in the schools deprive many Black deaf youth of the strong sense of racial pride many normally hearing Black young people have. This, added to educational deprivation and the communication difficulties which are inherent in deafness, leaves the problems of Black deaf people desperately in need of the attention Mr. Hairston's and Mr. Smith's book gives them.

Both authors are Black and deaf themselves and know intimately of the experiences and needs of which they write. In the pages which follow, they unfold a story large in human terms, if small relative to the number of people involved.

McCay Vernon, Ph.D
Editor, *American Annals of the Dcaf*

One More Time Again . . .

$This$ book developed as a result of our being invited periodically to speak on the subject of Black deaf people. After a while it became quite tiresome and our viewpoints constantly changed with time and events. Thus, to retain objectivity and suppress personal biases, we were forced to be more pragmatic.

In April 1972, at the 4th Biennial Conference of Professional Rehabilitation Workers with the Adult Deaf, we were among a panel composed of four Black deaf professionals in the areas of education and rehabilitation. We stated some of the major problems and concerns of Black deaf persons. Among the points brought out at the conference were:

1. Unemployment rates for Black deaf persons are much higher than for white deaf persons.

2. Very few Black deaf persons go beyond the eighth grade in school.

3. Black deaf persons and their parents are often not aware of the facilities or services that are available to them; information on continuing education, scholarships, or training programs bypasses them.

4. Because there are so few Black deaf professionals in the field of education and rehabilitation, most Black deaf children have no model to emulate and are given no inspiration to succeed.

Since then, quite a few studies have been made, at least one national survey has been conducted and reported in the *National Census of the Deaf Population,* and several articles on the Black deaf have appeared in various publications, including *PRWAD Deafness Annual III, The Deaf American,* and some conference reports.

Most of these reports, including our own, pointed out that the major problems faced by Black deaf people are undereducation and underemployment, which result in poor communication skills, low socioeconomic status, and an unfavorable self-image. This, although true, is an *oversimplification* of the problem, an easy way to explain away the plight of a handicapped minority, and a generalization that is hard to refute.

Let us again look at the two main problems: undereducation and underemployment. Although more prevalent among the deaf minorities, the Blacks,

American Indians, Chicanos, and Puerto Ricans, they also hold true for the general white deaf population. Are they really problems or are they simply life situations that need remedying?

About a year or so ago, we came across an article which opened with this statement:

> "The problems of the Black deaf, due to their unique status as a minority within a minority, result in a *bleak* picture of a *multi-disadvantaged group* characterized by *poverty, social isolation, gross lack of communication skills, unemployment* and *undereducation* . . . such a sad state of affairs."
>
> (italics ours)

This is a classic example of stereotyping or blanketing. However, to the author's credit, he did go on to document his findings, quote well known authorities, and provide statistical data. This is how *facts* could interfere with *truths*, they are not always synonymous where deafness and racial issues are concerned.

It is easy to assume that by using the term "Black deaf," one is grouping into a collective whole all the people who share the basic similarities of (a) being Black and (b) being deaf. The term, as used by the layman, not only includes the true similarities shared by members of this particular segment of the deaf population, but also attempts to formulate a set of rules or laws that are believed to describe or predict the behavior of all or most members of this population (i.e. "the Black deaf" are low verbal, etc.).

While certain similarities are shared by the majority of this group, it is not an entirely homogeneous group. Individual differences exist with regard to intelligence, social sophistication, etc. Generalizing or stereotyping about this subgroup of the deaf population can present many barriers to helping individual members, particularly with respect to the planning of educational programs and the effective use of such supportive services as rehabilitation and guidance. On the other hand, using the term "Black deaf" may be considered acceptable when one is attempting to focus attention on this group in an effort to help alleviate some of the problems faced by its members. It is in this respect that the term is used throughout this book.

As mentioned in the beginning, it is difficult to remain objective, especially if you're involved. We cannot help observing how well some of our "undereducated" Black deaf friends live and cannot overlook the fact that many seem to communicate and socialize well, in their fashion.

What, then, is the problem? The problem is mostly race related as well as attitudinal. Even today, some Black deaf people think that certain jobs are for whites only. They remain suspicious of professional service workers who try to help them improve their mode of living. Some employers are reluctant to hire Black deaf workers in other than routine or minimal jobs due to preconceived notions that they are incompetent. Some professional workers still believe that Black deaf persons are only able to do so much, thus are not too keen on helping them to realize their full potential or to obtain the necessary training for advancement or promotion.

Socially, one tends to mistakenly view the Black deaf as being isolated and/or inferior. Society has for a long time delegated them to a role of inferiority, thus some actually believe they are inferior.

Black deaf individuals seldom socialize freely and on an equal basis with the white deaf population. Exceptions may occur during their school years (if integrated) and during major athletic events among deaf clubs and associations. However, only a few Black deaf persons attend scheduled social affairs held after athletic events. Most get together with "their own" and have separate functions. It can be surmised that this situation is due to the differing social and cultural backgrounds of the groups and to the fact that one is most at ease among individuals like himself. Individual exceptions occur, of course, and in fact some Blacks prefer to associate only with whites.

The degree of communication skills that the average Black deaf person develops, as compared with those of the average white deaf person, in many ways accounts for his/her being snubbed and rejected in the deaf social and cultural milieu. Apparently, this rejection leads to a kind of segregation in reverse. To a degree, it forces one to find solace and companionship with his/her own organizations and social groups. Do we call this isolation? No! No more so than a gathering of professionals seeking companionship with like kind. Members of a minority group usually are isolated from society in general and, where deafness is present, they become even more so.

This book, then, is for the present and future generations—the children—to digest and to ask themselves, "Are we really different?" It is our belief that other than race related issues, the needs and problems of Black deaf persons are similar to those of deaf persons in general—educationally, vocationally, and socially.

To dismiss the racial aspect of deafness would be naive and presumptuous because the Black deaf person is already at a disadvantage from the time he is born. It can't be explained away and it won't go away easily. Attitudes die hard. Black deaf individuals have seldom been provided with a good educational foundation and with upward mobility opportunities to do meaningful work and to grow on the job. We live in a "hearing" and "color-conscious" society. We have only to look at the hearing world to see that we are lagging. The Reverend Jesse Jackson in one of his Project EXCEL speeches put it in perspective when he said:

> "There is one white attorney for every 680 whites, one Black attorney for every 4,000 Blacks; one white physician for every 649 whites, one Black physician for every 5,000 Blacks; one white dentist for every 1,900 whites, one Black dentist for every 8,400 Blacks. Less than 1 percent of all engineers are Black. Blacks make up less than 1 percent of all practicing chemists."

This book, we hope, will be a source of inspiration for school age Black deaf children who constantly need positive materials and models to "carry them through."

Too many of our young Black deaf children leave school without any knowledge of their heritage, without any pride in themselves, and without knowing what strengths they have that can be used in making a living and becoming self-respecting, contributing members of society.

Few school programs for the deaf contain information on Black history. Few Black deaf children have been exposed to Black deaf teachers, or for that matter, to Black deaf professionals or para-professional persons until they leave school. Most publications on deafness contain very little beneficial information on Black people which would be meaningful to Black deaf youth.

For parents and teachers we hope this book will prove meaningful and have a positive impact on everyone in the family and in the classroom. We are indebted to the people in the book who have bared their lives to reveal some truths, in hopes that their experiences will help children and young adults construct their future aspirations in a more rewarding way. We hope to light a fire for change.

Information about Black deaf people, written from a Black deaf perspective, has long been neglected in the development of Black deaf youth. This book will have served its purpose if it contributes to the eradication of this neglect.

Ernest E. Hairston
Linwood D. Smith

The Black Deaf Child and the Family

The birth of a deaf child into the family can be a traumatic experience or it can be a blessing, depending on the manner in which the condition is received. Early acceptance of the child's deafness is a crucial factor in his further development.

When a child is born deaf or becomes deaf early in life, many parents experience a strong sense of guilt and feelings of shame and desperation. Their concerns may or may not be realistic. They imagine the severe conditions under which the child will grow into maturity, the limitations of living in a world without sound, and the difficulties of intra-family communication.

Some parents try to overcompensate for these fears by overprotecting the deaf child and by gearing the entire family to accommodate the needs of the child, or they may go to the opposite extreme of ignoring the child altogether.

As the infant grows into babyhood the parents of the deaf child notice that he or she does not respond as hearing children do. Coping with a baby who responds to vibration and physical contact, as opposed to the spoken word, can be frustrating, especially for the mother who is most often left alone to deal with the deaf baby. Children seek parental attention, they are reinforced and encouraged to do so by parental feedback, either physical contact or spoken words. Even though they do not yet have the power of speech or a clear understanding of words, they can respond to imitation, gesture, and facial expression. The deaf child responds to both gesture and facial expression, but is not able to respond to the spoken word. This causes parents to feel frustrated because they realize they are unable to communicate with this smaller image of themselves. Children are the younger manifestation of ourselves. We see our lives relived through their eyes. When a deaf child is born into a hearing family, the parents of that child see someone different from themselves. This causes their inner emotions to overflow.

On discovering the child is deaf, usually the first professional person parents seek out for help is the family doctor. In most instances, medical doctors are not attuned to the psychological problems related to deafness. Most medical doctors after determining a hearing loss in the child then refer parents to an audiologist. The audiologist is trained in the non-medical measurement of hearing loss and prescribes hearing aids and rehabilitation. This is a critical period for parents who often forget their role at this time by acquiesing to the "professionals." However, this should be a time of mutual cooperation because parents are still the most important part of the child's life as children turn to them for understanding and help.

Children learn about racial differences very early in life. Deaf children are no exception. Black deaf children are exposed to the problems of racism early in school, in the community, and in family values and culture. This is good in that it broadens their perceptions and perspectives and enables most of them to better cope with life later on. On the other hand, does being Black really make any difference? Do Black parents have a harder time coping with deafness in the family than do other parents? The answer here can be two-pronged in that families on different socio-economic levels face things differently. As mentioned earlier, many Black families are usually burdened with making ends meet, raising a family, and coping with the ever changing world. They generally do not have sufficient time or energy to devote to the deaf child. And more often than not, they do not know where to turn for help. Although this sounds like discredited folklore, it is still true to the extent that few cities are as fortunate as the Washington, D.C. metropolitan area where an organization, *Parents for Deafpride,* is operating. Deafpride seems to be a boon to parents with deaf and hard-of-hearing children, especially in inner city areas where professional help is scarce. It offers counseling, prenatal care, advocacy, and communication services for parents and deaf children. Parents are much better able to cope when they can share their experiences with other parents. This is often better than individual counseling. In many rural areas, this may prove to be an impossibility for families whose child may be the only deaf person in the area. Most states have a state school for the deaf where parent counseling and communication services should be available.

As children grow we begin to expect things of them. With deaf children many parents wonder just what to expect. When we expect little of deaf children, most likely we will get little, and when we expect a lot, chances are we will get a lot. Because the child is deaf is no reason to have low expectations of their abilities and capabilities. Many deaf people have high expectations of themselves. Many Black deaf people are the only persons in their family to attend and graduate from college.

In speaking of Black families, we find that they are very unique, quite different from other families in that many Black families are similar and have many strengths. Robert Hill, author of *The Strengths of Black Families,* analyzed the manner in which Black families have been able to survive and move beyond survival to a high level of existence in our society. Hill notes the five basic Black family strengths:

1. Strong Kinship Bonds
   (The absorption of individuals, minors, elderly, and handicapped)

2. Strong Work Orientation

3. Adaptability of Family Roles

4. High Achievement Orientation

5. Strong Religious Orientation

Specifically, Black people want to work. Some Black parents have two or three jobs just so their children will have a better life than themselves. They want to achieve educationally and economically. They have strong spiritual values. Black deaf children when exposed to these things come to feel a part of the family. They learn family values, goals, and expectations.

This is a form of communication at its best and the Black deaf child should be part of this sharing in the joy and sorrow of everyday family life. It is hard to overstate the importance of spending time with the deaf child and not treating him any differently than any other child in the family. Parents should be there to share their moments of happiness and defeat, to lend words of encouragement, to say "no" when necessary, and to recognize the frustration many Black deaf children experience.

In 1971, McCay Vernon and Eugene Mindel published *They Grow in Silence,* one of the most widely read and praised books on the deaf child and the family. They hoped that the book would help overcome some of the failures of communication between parents and professionals. Vernon and Mindel view the goal of effective family communication as being the key to the mature development of the child. *They Grow in Silence* is aimed at helping parents and professionals to understand deafness and its ramifications so that the problems can be viewed in their entirety rather than in isolated aspects.

No two children are alike. Each child, each family is different and has different needs. Parental expectations and involvement vary, some are very demanding, some want little or nothing. The key in working with families is to focus on the child as an individual, as a deaf person with his own unique personality, strengths, values, and abilities, and to go from there—upwards!

Education: Black
Deaf Students

Where We've Been

Approximately two million Blacks have a hearing impairment serious enough to require special medical or educational services. Of this two million approximately 22,000 are profoundly deaf.

Early profound deafness is said to be the most severe handicap a child can have because he is denied the most vital developmental stimulus of all—the voice. Deafness is also a severe educational handicap. A glaring characteristic of the education most deaf school graduates receive is their low achievement and reading levels.

Historically and traditionally, the education of Black deaf children, as with Black children in general, has been of a second-class nature—a game in which they started late and are still trying to catch up.

When speaking of the education of Black deaf children, it is necessary to take a backward look in order to understand the present situation. In researching for information on education involving Black deaf children during the pre-integration days, we interviewed several of our older acquaintances to solicit their views on their educational background and what the system was like when they started out. We talked to "J" who was deafened by spinal meningitis at seven years of age, transferred from public school to a Southern school for the Negro deaf, and started all over again at grade one. He spent eight years in that program and, through luck, transferred to a private religious preparatory school. Even if he had stayed at the school for the Negro deaf a few years longer, he would not have graduated. "Graduation was something unheard of in this separate program for Blacks and was only known to happen in the dual system reserved for whites," he bitterly remarked years later. Not fully benefitting from the prep school because of his deafness, he moved to a Northern city and attended the school for the deaf there. At that school he received some vocational training, participated in sports, and got a reasonable secondary education. When asked what were some significant events affecting him that contributed to his success in life, he responded:

> While at the (Southern) school, I was fortunate to have had a deaf teacher who was very civic minded and with good insight into the needs and learning problems of the deaf students. This person happened to be white (Blacks were not hired as instructors at that school then) and very much dedicated to his teaching as were most of the

9

Scenes of classroom and dormitory buildings at the School for the Deaf and Blind, Overlea, Maryland. Black deaf persons from Maryland and the Washington metropolitan area attended this school before the deaf department was phased out in the 1950's.

teachers who were deaf. As I now recall, this teacher had a very touching and dramatic way of arousing self-awareness in the students and (awareness of) the world around them. This teacher was a great factor in my later curiousity about myself as a Black person in the world and my later interest in doing outside reading beyond that called for in class.

While at the (Northern) school, the great civil rights movement was just starting to take place. Jackie Robinson had just broken into major league baseball, the U.S. Supreme Court had ordered the University of Texas to admit its first Black student, and other sweeping changes were taking place in our government. After classes I was reading just about every bit of news the civil rights movement made and felt a strong identification with it. This was a factor in my eventually applying for admission to Gallaudet College which theretofore had no Black deaf students in its program. My application was accepted but I failed to pass the examination for admission for the obvious reason that the school was reluctant to push, or to be a party in pushing for, integration at Gallaudet College by placing me in the class with the other college bound students from the school. However, after some protest and another try, I was fortunate to become the second Black student accepted at Gallaudet.

When last interviewed, "J" was a successful vocational adjustment instructor in a school for the deaf. And he had earned his Masters degree the year before.

For more than a century and a half, deaf children have been educated in special schools in America, yet Black deaf children, especially those in Southern states, have been relegated to segregated schools, just as have their hearing peers.

Many Blacks have attended schools for the deaf for 13 years or more, only to graduate with a second to fourth grade achievement level or less. This was especially true of the previously segregated schools in the South; however, the Northern schools have not done much better.

In the South, most of these schools were jointly for deaf and blind students and were called state schools for the "Colored or Negro" deaf and blind, such as North Carolina School for the Negro Deaf and Blind, Florida School for the Negro Deaf and Blind. In the early 1950's, 13 states were operating separate and segregated schools for the deaf. As late as 1963, eight states maintained separate facilities.

Gallaudet College, established in 1864 and the world's only liberal arts college for the deaf, did not open its door to Black students until about 1952. By 1964, Gallaudet's Centennial year, only a handful of Black deaf persons had graduated. Even though they were educated, professional, and admired by other Black deaf persons, most had no role model that they could emulate and were rarely encouraged to aspire to anything higher than classroom teaching.

A researcher at Gallaudet College's Learning Center (D. DeLorenzo) stated that Hume Le P. Battiste, Class of 1913, was the first Black deaf graduate of Gallaudet College. This caused controversy. Not the question of whether or not Battiste graduated, but whether or not he was Black. Some say he was Indian, some say Creole. Papers, however, seem to indicate that he was Black. If this is so, then other questions rear their curious heads. Did he 'pass for white' in order to enter Gallaudet?

HUME LE P BATTISTE
PENNA.

Copy of a letter from A. C. Manning to E. M. Gallaudet, dated August 24, 1908. It hints that Battiste was Black. However, further research revealed that he was of Indian descendent. (The case is not yet firm). *Courtesy of Gallaudet College Archives.*

Waleska, Ga.
Aug. 24, 1908.

Dr. E. M. Gallaudet,
Washington, D.C.
My dear Dr. Gallaudet,
I want to speak to you in behalf of Mr. Hume Battiste, one of our recent graduates at the Mt. Airy School. Last spring he took the College examinations and was admitted into your Introductory Class. But he is considered a Negro and there's the rub.

2.

The report is being circulated that the College boys intend to make it so disagreeable for him in case he enters college that he can't stay. He appeals to me for advice and I know of no better course than to lay the case before you.

You know I am a Southern man with all the senti- ments so frequently called "race prejudice", but I want to assure you that this young man is one of the most interesting boys I ever taught and so far³ is he above the average you naturally never think of his racial misfortunes. During the past year I taught him and found him to be an excellent character, possessing rare qualities,—nor is he at all offensive in appearance or manner.

His ambition is to become a pharmacist and I also desire to have you advise him on this point. Not being acquainted with a deaf pharmacist, I hardly knew whether or not to encourage him in this hope. His mother does not

want him to attend College
unless there is a possibil-
ity of his becoming a
pharmacist, as he already
has a good trade at which
he can make a living.

I hope the young man
may receive favorable con-
sideration, for I believe he
will prove himself
worthy.

Hoping that the summer's
vacation has done you
much good, I remain
            Yours respectfully,
            A.C. Manning

Did Gallaudet knowingly admit a Black person when segregation was in force? If Blacks were admitted to Gallaudet in the early years, when did the doors close on them and why?

"T" is a counselor with a rehabilitation program in Indianapolis, Indiana, and for over 30 years was a volunteer para-professional with organizations serving the deaf and with community service agencies. During the same period, "T" worked at an electronics company. When we asked if he ever applied for college, he replied:

> The reason I did not go to Gallaudet College was because, prior to 1949, educational programs were segregated in Washington, D.C., which also included Gallaudet College. I was informed in my sophomore year at the Indiana School for the Deaf that Blacks were not allowed to go to Gallaudet. Four of us Black students did not know what to do after we learned this. Naturally, I lost interest in studying with no goals for which to aim. Going to Gallaudet used to be my number one goal since many ISD graduates went there . . .

Today, things are far different. Gains were made mostly through street demonstrations and court actions brought on by Blacks in general and their invaluable white sympathizers. Black deaf people played little or no role in such demonstrations, but reaped the benefits that resulted. When schools became integrated or desegregated, few if any provisions were made for the disadvantaged backgrounds and special needs of Black deaf children. At least, in segregated schools there is little if any identity problem, social discrimination, or "benign neglect."

In the late 1940's and throughout the 1950's, most schools for the Negro or colored placed strong emphasis on vocational training and skills and made certain most of their graduates were employed. The West Virginia School for the Colored Deaf and Blind, for example, prior to integrating with the West Virginia School for the Deaf and Blind in Romney, offered its students training in home economics, typing, tailoring, pressing (dry cleaning), beauty culture (hairdressing), barbering, and shoe repairing. "Programmed" is a better description than "offered" since students were placed in training programs according to grade, age, and mental ability rather than by aptitude and each student, no matter what his or her intelligence level, was allowed to try and become proficient in at least two vocations. For example, from age 12 to 14, it was tailoring and pressing for boys; typing, cooking, or sewing for girls. From 15 to 21, depending on when they graduated from school, courses were barbering, shoe repairing, or dry cleaning for boys and home economics and continuing beauty culture for girls. The West Virginia School for the Colored Deaf was located in close proximity to West Virginia State College, an all-Black college at that time and most of the vocational teachers were also teachers at the college. For instance, the barber teacher, who taught at the deaf school, was also head of the barber college at West Virginia State; the tailoring teacher had his own shop near campus and taught at the deaf school from two to four in the afternoons, as most of the other vocational teachers did.

Four of six vocational instructors were master craftsmen and demanded quality work from their students. Consequently, when the students graduated, whether with a vocational certificate, diploma, or both, they had a marketable skill and were usually placed in employment shortly after. Most popular were barbering and tailoring for boys and beauty culture for girls. Some eventually became shopowners. Students in barbering and beauty culture were required to take the examinations of the State Board of Barbers and Beauticians. Upon passing, they received licenses to work for one year as apprentices and then as master barbers or beauticians. The state presented them with the tools of the trade.

In most of the other Southern states, schools for the Negro deaf and blind were usually near predominantly Black colleges from which many vocational and academic teachers and dormitory personnel were recruited. The Louisiana School was near Southern University, the North Carolina School was near Shaw University, and the Virginia School was near Hampton Institute. These schools prided themselves on their vocational training record; the academic side was also strongly emphasized, albeit less successfully. For example, the course of study at the West Virginia School for the Colored Deaf and Blind in 1951 was as follows:

Academic Program of the Deaf

The education of a deaf child presents much greater difficulties than that of the blind. It is the consensus of opinion that the training of a congenitally deaf child is the supreme challenge to teaching skills. When such a child enters school at five (5) or six (6) years of age, he is usually devoid of any concept of language. He frequently does not know his own name nor the names of any of the objects with which he has had contact. His only method of communication is by means of grunts, noises, cries, and simple gestures. He looks out upon a world that he sees and touches but cannot interpret to others nor have interpreted to himself through the common medium of spoken language. Soon after he enters school, he is also taken to a specialist in Charleston for an examination to determine the degree of his hearing loss. The audiogram, or chart of the loss of hearing in decibels, is kept on file as a guide in the child's training. His loss may be of a slight degree and thus his hearing can be improved by the use of a mechanical aid.

Thus, as the result of a lack of language caused by inability to hear the spoken word, the deaf child begins his school career at a great disadvantage. For two or three years the teacher labors unceasingly to give the little deaf child the rudiments of language before he can even reach the stage of the hearing child at the beginning of the first grade. This retardation of two or three years because of the language handicap can seldom be overcome. The deaf pupil throughout his educational career remains two, three, or more grades behind his normal brothers and sisters of the same age.

Two basic methods have prevailed in the education of the deaf. The one is the Oral Method and the other the Normal Method. There may be combinations of the two. However, the best schools of our country employ the Oral Method exclusively, and the time is not far distant when all the schools will follow that method. In the oral method, the deaf child is taught to make sounds, to speak, and to understand speech by reading the movement of the lips, jaws, and face. It is a long, slow, difficult process and calls for the utmost skill and patience on the part of the teacher. The manual method makes use of signs and fingerspelling. This is the universal language of the deaf and has come down through the years. The one serious drawback to this method is that so few normal persons understand the sign language.

This school has sought to use a combination of the two methods, with the emphasis placed upon the oral approach. The chief difficulty encountered has been the lack of teachers trained in the oral method. However, that situation has improved greatly in recent years.

Speech and language remain the important subjects for a deaf student throughout most of his school career. Therefore, fewer of the deaf than the blind have finished the high school course. The vast majority complete the eighth or ninth grades along with a vocation and are then able to make their way to success in life. The curricular offerings in the deaf department show some variations from those of the regular public schools.

An outline of the course of study in the Deaf Department follows.

Course of Study

DEAF DEPARTMENT

PREPARATORY
DEPARTMENT:
A. First Year
   1. Preparatory sense training
   2. Speech
   3. Speechreading
   4. Language
   5. Handwork
   6. Number work
B. Second Year
   1. Sense training
   2. Speech
   3. Speechreading
   4. Number work
   5. Language
   6. Reading

PRIMARY
DEPARTMENT:
A. First Grade
   1. Speech
   2. Language
   3. Reading
   4. Number work
   5. Social work
   6. Hand work
   7. Sense training
B. Second Grade
   1. Speech
   2. Sense Training
   3. Language
   4. Reading
   5. Arithmetic
   6. Hand work
   7. Speechreading
C. Third Grade
   1. Speech
   2. Speechreading
   3. Language
   4. Reading
   5. Arithmetic
   6. Social Studies
   7. Hand work

INTERMEDIATE
DEPARTMENT:
A. Fourth Grade
   1. Speech
   2. Reading
   3. Language
   4. Arithmetic
   5. Geography
   6. History
   7. Industrial Arts
B. Fifth Grade
   1. Speechreading
   2. Language
   3. Arithmetic
   4. Health
   5. Geography
   6. History
   7. Industrial Arts
   8. Science
   9. Reading
C. Sixth Grade
   1. Speechreading
   2. Language
   3. Arithmetic
   4. Reading
   5. Geography
   6. History
   7. Health
D. Seventh Grade
   1. Speechreading
   2. English
   3. History
   4. Geography

5. Arithmetic
6. Health
7. Reading

ADVANCED
DEPARTMENT:

A. Eighth Grade
   1. Speechreading
   2. English
   3. Civics
   4. History
   5. Current Events
   6. Reading
   7. Mathematics
   8. Hygiene
B. Ninth Grade
   1. Speechreading
   2. English
   3. General Science
   4. History
   5. Current Events

6. Mathematics
7. Hygiene

C. Tenth Grade
   1. Speechreading
   2. English and Literature
   3. Algebra
   4. History
   5. Science
D. Eleventh Grade
   1. Speechreading
   2. English and Literature
   3. Biology
   4. Science
   5. History
E. Twelth Grade
   1. Algebra
   2. English
   3. History
   4. Literature
   5. Current Events

The foregoing example is by no means the model that all, nor even the majority of, schools for the Black deaf followed. Some schools, as stated earlier, did not even award certificates to some of their students. The most unfortunate aspect of this situation was that students with higher than average intelligence were deprived of or denied opportunities to achieve higher than a secondary education. A few, however, did manage to enroll in and graduate from Black public colleges. On the other hand, there were no available jobs to match their educational level.

On May 17, 1954, the Supreme Court ruled that the separate-but-equal doctrine (Plessy *vs* Ferguson) used to exclude Black children from public schools maintained for white children was unconstitutional. However, many school administrators sought to prevent Blacks from enrolling by stating that their schools were set up for "whites only" or that they were for the most part "privately" supported.

The Court did not require a deadline for desegregation efforts but did say that it should be carried out "with all deliberate speed." Problems immediately arose among schools relating to administration, the recruitment and integration of additional staff, and physical plants and transportation. With the desegregation of most of the Southern schools during the 1960's, Black deaf children were assimilated into previously predominantly white institutions. With their admittance into these schools, Black deaf children for the most part became cultural nonentities.

The entire staff at the West Virginia School for the Colored Deaf and Blind in 1951. From left to right: Mrs. Olivia Strader, Miss Elizabeth Hendrick, Mrs. Mamie Anderson, Miss Emily Raspberry, Mr. E. A. Bolling, Superintendent, Miss Gertrude Dunkley, Mrs. Edmonia Grider, Miss Minnie C. Holley, Principal, Mrs. Mamie Burks. Second row: Mr. Felix T. Warren, Mrs. Katherine B. Robinson, Mrs. Maggie Moore, Mr. William King, Miss Marion Williams, Mrs. W. W. Sanders, Mr. R. J. McCollum, Mr. Jerry Lee. Mr. Fred Sawyers, not in the picture.

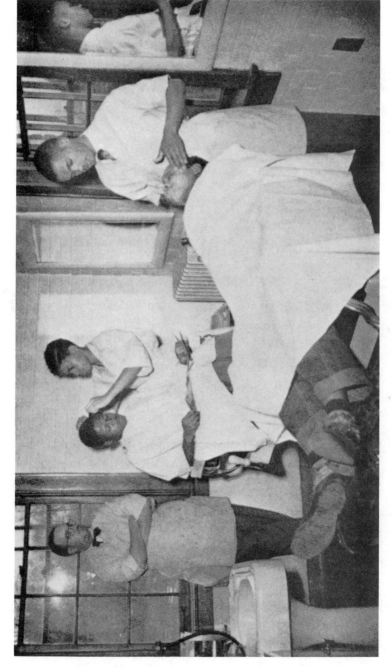

The Barber Shop
Mr. Felix T. Warren, Instructor

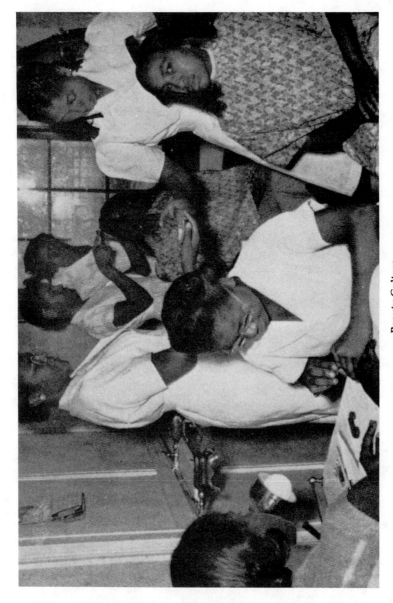

Beauty Culture
Miss Minnie C. Holley, Instructor

Cleaning and Pressing Department

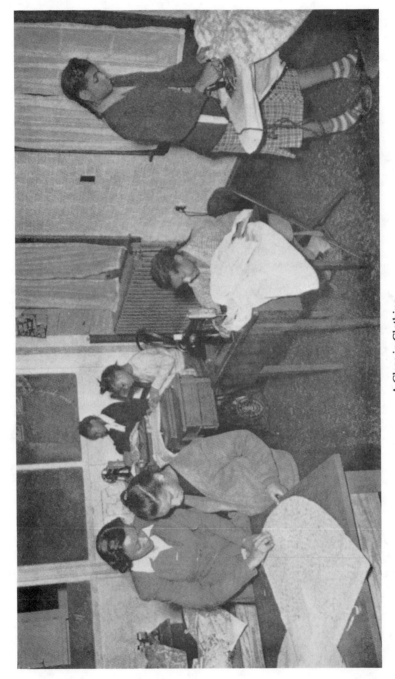

A Class in Clothing
Mrs. Edmonia W. Grider, Instructor

24

Deaf and Blind Arts and Craft Class
Mrs. Katherine B. Robinson, Instructor

25

Gymnasium and Auditorium

Where We Are Now

Today, a basic education is a necessity. It is viewed by many as a barrier breaker, a key to open doors that would otherwise be closed. Since the early 1960's, the field of education of the deaf has grown with the emergence of new programs, innovations, technology, and manpower. More educational, vocational, and employment opportunities for deaf persons have been provided by the National Technical Institute for the Deaf in Rochester, New York; the Technical Vocational Institute in Saint Paul, Minnesota; the Center on Deafness and the Leadership Training Program in the area of deafness at California State University, Northridge, California; the Deafness Research and Training Center at New York University; and other postsecondary programs.

It was mentioned previously that many Black deaf children are already at a disadvantage by the time they enter school. The needs of the child will vary according to his or her background and intelligence. However, when most deaf children complete school, there is still a need for continuing education to reinforce basic language, social, everyday living, and vocational skills. Black deaf people are becoming more aware of and visible in continuing education, adult education, vocational education, and postsecondary school programs. In increasing numbers, they are becoming role models for a new generation of Black deaf children.

In their book, *The Deaf Population of the United States*, Schein and Delk report some interesting educational statistics that have rarely been taken into account in most research concerning Black deaf people. They reported that of their sample of non-white deaf people. . . .

> ". . . the non-white male had the lowest median grade (10.1), only 17% reported completing high school, with 60% below the 12th grade. But nearly 23% complete one or more years of college . . . non-white females had the highest proportion that finished high school, but the smallest completing one or more years of college. The median grade attained by non-white females (11.4) was the highest of both white and non-white males and females."

These statistics say that non-white females achieve further in school but not many go on to college.

In the field of Education, one of the more far reaching laws in recent years to have impact on the education of *all* handicapped children is Public Law 94-142. This is also known as the "Education for All Handicapped Children Act of 1975." Some of the most important parts of this law affecting deaf children are:

1. For each handicapped child there will be an "Individualized Education Program" (IEP) that is a written statement of the child's educational goals developed by both parents and teachers.

2. Handicapped and non-handicapped children will be educated together as much as possible.

3. Tests and evaluation material used in placing handicapped children will be given in such a way as not to be racially or culturally discriminating and in a language which both the parent and child can understand.

27

4. Before the school tests a child or changes his educational program, the parents must be informed and have given prior approval.

5. Special efforts will be made to employ qualified handicapped persons.

No law is a good law unless it is enforced. From the language and implications of Public Law 94-142, it is obvious that parents will have to play a major role in taking the initiative and leading the attack to ensure that equal educational opportunities for their child are made a reality. Our assumption is that many Black deaf students, parents, and school personnel are not fully aware of the law, its provisions, and its implications. However, as detailed in *Deafness Annual III, 1977*, pp. 197–98, the authors note that many Black families have other obstacles to overcome, working from day to day to make ends meet and to provide wholesome home lives for their children. Only a few Black parents have the time and resources to vigorously pursue their rights and those of their handicapped children.

Another major concern in the field of deafness has been the trend toward mainstreaming deaf children into classes with regular hearing students. Proponents of mainstreaming believe that a higher degree of normality results when deaf and hearing children are placed in the same classes. Although this is not necessarily true, such programs do in many instances allow the child to attend school closer to home and are said to be better for the child's overall social development. Individual differences should, again, be considered. For some Black deaf children, being educated in a residential school setting may provide more appropriate educational experiences than a mainstreamed program. Options should be offered. The education of Black deaf children must rely on concerned teachers, parents, and others who vigorously demand quality educational programs and maximum results for each individual child. Black deaf children deserve no less.

Rehabilitation and the Black Deaf Person

Generally speaking, vocational rehabilitation agencies have played major roles in advancing the social and economic well-being of many deaf people. This is especially true where Black deaf persons from low socioeconomic backgrounds are concerned. Evidence of this kept appearing during our interviews with Black deaf adults. Often they were the only family member to attend college or to have skilled or semi-skilled jobs, such as barbering, tailoring, or hairdressing. Usually it was a direct result of training obtained at schools for the deaf and subsequent jobs obtained with help from state vocational rehabilitation agencies, and, in the case of college, a tuition-paid education. Jobs for Blacks within the printing industry and the U.S. Postal Service came later.

Unless they received scholarships, their Black hearing peers would either join the armed services or work at unskilled jobs. This was the picture during the 1950's and early 1960's. During the late 1960's and 1970's, the whole civil rights scene changed and affected a broad spectrum of people—ethnic minorities, handicapped, and women. At many segregated schools for the Negro deaf, emphasis was on vocational rather than academic training and the average age of "graduates" was 20. It constituted a picture of an underprivileged deaf person, tired of school, highly trained in a vocation (shoe repair, tailoring, barbering, or hairdressing) or fully prepared to become a homemaker. Few, very few, had the desire to continue their education. Nearly all of them were eager to begin work immediately after graduation.

Some people just refused to fit the mold. One such is a close friend of the authors. She attended, as a teenager, a school for the Negro deaf in the Deep South. Unlike most students in that school, she had spunk and expressed her opinions, not in a belligerent way. To illustrate, when she was 16 years of age, she thought she had learned all she could from that school and was ready to graduate. The principal did not agree, but being a fair and considerate person, he compromised.

They agreed that she would take the Gallaudet College Entrance Examination and, if she passed, she would graduate from high school. She graduated. With invaluable financial assistance from her State Bureau of Vocational Rehabilitation, she went on to become the only member of her family to graduate from college. Fifteen years later, a brother duplicated her accomplishment.

Ten years later, Carolyn McCaskill, one of our interviewees, a newly desegregated school attendee after some years at segregated schools, was asked, "What is it like to be Black and deaf?" She answered, "Lucky." Although not true in most cases, the number of Blacks who benefited from college educations, solid vocational training in one or two vocations, or similar special services is significant in that they would not have succeeded if they were not deaf.

One major problem is the disparity in vocational rehabilitation policies from state to state. During the segregation and early integration era, most vocational rehabilitation agencies in Southern states provided financial assistance for only four years to clients attending college, regardless of how many years it took the client to obtain his degree. The majority of students attending Gallaudet require five years to complete their degrees, the first year being the preparatory class. Several Black deaf students from economically strapped families suffered during their senior year, unless they received one or more scholarships.

On the other hand, some of the larger and richer states were generous with their support to the point of paying substantial monthly allowances. The fact one had to maintain passing grades in order to receive continued support was good. However, consider this situation where one would continuously make the Dean's List for four years. Then, before the beginning of the fifth and final year, one is informed that he or she or the parents would have to continue the financing because state-supported financing is terminated. Such decisions had nothing to do with a person's race. They cut across racial lines. Blacks, being at or near the bottom of the economic ladder, were more directly affected. Among the deaf population, persons who benefit most from vocational rehabilitation services are those fortunate enough to attend and graduate from postsecondary or other types of training programs, other than pre-vocational.

However, a majority of deaf individuals who seek or are in need of rehabilitative services are not so fortunate. Since there is no such thing as an average client and no two clients are alike, a composite sketch would be a school for the deaf attendee, possessing minimal verbal skills, undecided about the type of job or training desired, or with hopes of obtaining a high paying job right away. When visiting a counselor's office, usually at the urging of friends or relatives, he is given forms to be filled, instructions to obtain a general medical examination, and even a psychological examination among others. Then he is told to return in, say, two weeks. Upon returning with forms properly filled, he may be referred for vocational/occupational evaluation or, if lucky, placed in a job usually below his potential. The result is often frustration and distrust for the rehabilitative process. This is not true in all cases, not even in most cases, but it happens often enough to attract attention.

With the concept of the Individualized Written Rehabilitation Program (IWRP), introduced by the enactment of the Rehabilitation Act of 1973, this situation may be averted to some extent. The Individualized Written Rehabilitation Program, however, is being interpreted differently by individual states and is too new a concept to be effectively evaluated. In the meantime, the burden remains with the counselor, his ability to communicate with the client well enough, and his patience to explain the rehabilitation process in terms of the following steps:

1. the necessity of determining eligibility for services,

2. the time required to find an appropriate job and rationale for "temporary" underemployment, and

3. the need for further training or evaluation, whichever is the case.

Harry Whiting, Jr., in "Services to Black Deaf Adults", stated:

> ". . . . it was found to be true that not only are the Black deaf reluctant to go
> to DVR for services, but also that they may be reluctant to see a counselor
> who is able to communicate with the deaf, but is a white person. Because
> many Black deaf persons have not had the opportunity to be SERVED BY A
> BLACK PERSON (deaf, hard-of-hearing, hearing), they lack the inspiration
> to succeed and grow with society. Black people have few professional models
> to emulate. . . No matter how hard a white person (deaf, hard-of-hearing, or
> hearing) tries, the Black deaf generally will not accept him or her as a part of
> them."

Was this reluctance due to the fact that the counselor was white?
Maybe, in part. It could also be due to the fact that Black deaf clients have been
rebuffed so many times and placed in stereotyped employment or training situations,
or were simply unaware of opportunities open to them. Thus, they considered vocational rehabilitation help a waste of time. We do not think normal Black deaf persons
will have problems relating to a counselor who shows genuine empathy along with
the ability to communicate.

The plight of many Black deaf persons, rehabilitation-wise, is com-
parable to a neglected section of the deaf population. Dr. Boyce Williams and Edna
Adler, in an unpublished document, described them as follows:

> A large neglected population of deaf youth and adults which has been esti-
> mated to be from 50,000 to 100,000 individuals. Since most of them have
> normal strength, mobility, and intelligence, the large majority can be trained
> for independent living as has already been proved in research demonstrations.
> They are the unfortunates who are known as 16 years or older deaf people
> whose maximum vocational potential has not been achieved. While the large
> portion of these people have only the single disability of deafness with its
> myriad handicapping aspects, numbers do have other disabilities, such as
> cerebral palsy, limited vitality, visual defect, orthopedic involvement, and so
> on. These secondary disabilities only complicate but do not at all preclude the
> effectiveness of appropriate training. This whole population has great diffi-
> culty in entering and holding suitable employment because each person man-
> ifests combinations of the following six clusters of characteristics:
>
> > 1. *Unsatisfactory educational experience*
> >   Many of these people have had no formal education.
> >   Others have not benefited from brief or even extensive
> >   educational exposure for complex reasons that could
> >   include lack of readiness, behavioral problems, improper
> >   teaching methods, family circumstances, and so on. Their
> >   functional level as measured in educational terms may
> >   be third grade or less.
> >
> > 2. *Very limited communication ability*
> >   Few of this population read and write at the third grade
> >   level. Many have very meager to no ability in reading
> >   and writing. Moreover, they usually offer very poor speech
> >   and speechreading abilities. Even their sign language
> >   abilities may be very inadequate.
> >
> > 3. *Insufficient daily living skills*
> >   Many of the people are unprepared, and thus unable, to
> >   live independently. They depend upon family, friends,

or custodial situations because they have not been trained in common routines, such as money, transportation, time, personal hygiene, health, marketing, cooking, and so on. Moreover, the frustrations attending such limitations compound their coping capacities resulting in seriously deficient behavior with people and environment.

4. *Social isolation*
Serious inadequacy in interpersonal relationships are very common in this population. Because of frequent rejection, even by family and other deaf people, they may manifest shyness, distrust, hostility, confusion leading to withdrawal from the supportive relationships that people need. As a consequence, they may be easy prey for begging rings, drug addiction, alcoholic excess, confidence men, and similar problems, with eventual or intermittent incarceration.

5. *Poor occupational history*
Because of their lack of training, they manifest poor work habits, immature behavior, rigidity, inflexibility, naivete in pay check deductions, job fringe benefits, promptness, vacation and other leave. Consequently, many have had limited or no full-time competitive employment. Such remunerative job experience as they may have had has usually been marginal at best, with pay at less than the poverty level in situations having great employee turnover.

6. *Unsatisfactory rehabilitation experience*
Substantial numbers of this population are or have been clients of the state vocational rehabilitation agencies. Because the highly specialized, intensive training that they need is not available and because the costs of establishing and maintaining an appropriate program for them is beyond the fiscal capability of any state alone, these clients remain unserved or in ineffective service delivery situations until they are closed as not feasible or as behavioral problems rooted in the frustrations attending unsatisfying daily experience.

On another document, *RSA FY 78-79 Major Initiative,* Williams wrote:

"In the period 1969–1973, the Department of HEW, through the Rehabilitation Services Administration, undertook the first National Census of the Deaf since the early 1930's. Conducted by the National Association of the Deaf, and the Deafness Research and Training Center at New York University, the Census of the Deaf reached the following major findings:

Prevocationally deaf persons work in every industry, a vast array of tasks. Deaf persons have demonstrated their ability to do almost any type of work.

The most clearcut measure of the penalty of deafness is personal income. The average annual income for employed deaf persons fell $2,273 below the comparable figure for the general population. The prevocationally deaf worker's average income is 72 percent of the general population average. The nonwhite deaf worker earns, on the average, only 62 percent as much as nonwhite workers in general.

Better than average earnings are associated with education and vocational rehabilitation. However, prevocationally deaf persons require specialized educational and rehabilitation assistance—commodities in short supply in many areas.

The census of the deaf concluded that "Swift, concerted action is called for, if the projected needs of these young deaf people are to be met successfully." The census also identified an alarming trend toward educating older deaf workers in areas of minimal utility.

"With respect to occupations, the deaf population is not well placed for the anticipated shift in the economy. Too many deaf workers hold jobs in declining industries or occupational categories. Vocational preparation can aid new deaf workers by directing them toward occupations for which demand will be great."

This indicates that more leadership needs to be provided from the Federal level to improve and expand services to the deaf. And the National Association of the Deaf should continue to play an important leadership role. Unfortunately, too few Black deaf persons, leaders or otherwise, are involved in sharing their insights into the specific needs of Black deaf people.

Clubs: The Gathering Places

It is often said that the club is the deaf person's second home. It has also been said that the club is the heart of the deaf community. It is at the club for the deaf where ideas are exchanged, friendships formed, dances held, the latest happenings in the community shared, and where certain members merge as leaders. For many Black deaf people it is the only opportunity to get together with other deaf people on a regular basis.

Over the years, there have been several clubs comprised wholly or predominantly of Black deaf people. Some have disbanded, some have merged with others, and some are still in existence. Several Black deaf leaders in various states early realized that Black deaf people desired to meet and to come together for social or political purposes. These early clubs met on street corners, in barber shops, at the YMCA, and in each other's homes.

One of the better known earlier clubs is the Washington Silent Society, a forerunner of the current Capital City Association of the Deaf. It was established shortly after World War II and continued through the early 1950's. Like many clubs and societies for Black deaf persons, the Washington Silent Society was established in part because Blacks were barred from participating in or joining the District of Columbia Association of the Deaf, forerunner of the present Metropolitan Washington Association of the Deaf.

Ironically, CCAD and MWAD are now housed only 12 blocks apart from each other and their membership rosters include persons of all races. However, CCAD remains predominantly Black while MWAD is predominantly white. This is more a result of choice than of design.

In an attempt by the members to attract, identify, and work with the large numbers of Black deaf adults in the District of Columbia as well as parents and deaf children in the Kendall School and the Model Secondary School for the Deaf, the CCAD Newsletter was established in July 1973 to keep the community informed on the activities of CCAD and to report other local and national news of interest.

Another well known club for Black deaf persons operating since the 1950's is the Lincoln Club for the Deaf in Chicago. During the early 1960's, several other clubs for Black deaf persons came into existence: the Blue Jay Club for the Deaf in Los Angeles, the Ebony Club for the Deaf in Atlanta, the Baltimore Silents Club, among others. Most of these clubs were formed mainly for social and athletic purposes. Main events were dances and sports competitions, such as softball and basketball.

37

Title Page of *The Lincoln News*, December, 1981 Lincoln Club for the Deaf, Chicago, Illinois

The women's rights movement of the 1970's also spurred a great deal of interest among Black deaf women in establishing clubs to address some of their needs. Women Unlimited of Washington, D.C., the Silent Chatterbox Club of Atlanta, and the Soul Sisters of Cleveland, Ohio, are clubs comprised of Black deaf women.

Women Unlimited is an organization of hearing-impaired and hearing women who share a common interest in promoting and maintaining the welfare of deaf women in the Washington metropolitan area. It was founded in 1974 by four deaf women with an interest in self-improvement and a desire to encourage other deaf women to aspire to increased self-awareness, self-confidence, and a more active involvement in community affairs through a variety of educational and social experiences.

Women Unlimited sponsors workshops for both members of the organization and the local community and strives to keep members informed and encourages them to take advantage of the educational, social, and cultural opportunities available to area residents. The organization contributes to the community social/cultural scene each year with events and programs planned for the public or a select group of citizens.

Soul Sisters is a social club for Black deaf women in Cleveland, Ohio, dedicated to the task of improving the social life of the Black deaf citizens of Cleveland. Soul Sisters was founded in 1975 by a group of women concerned with the social opportunities of Black deaf women in Cleveland. The members of the club meet biweekly, taking turns as hostesses in their homes. They plan dances, parties, and other social events.

Another club of note is the Ebony Harambee Club on the Gallaudet College campus. It is comprised of Gallaudet students and sponsors public affairs programs, dances, and lectures for the student body.

CCAD NEWS

Capital City Association of the Deaf   Vol. 1 No. 1
JULY, 1973

Dear Friends,

This issue marks the emergence of CCAD News, the paper of the Capital City Association of the Deaf. For the past ten years or so CCAD has focused its activities almost entirely on social and athletic affairs. While we are no less concerned with the importance of these we have grown into a responsible civic and community organization responding to the growing numbers of people who would like to know more about us, our aims, and about the black deaf in general.

While there are other organizations of black deaf people in the United States, the Capital City Association of the Deaf is unique in that it is located in the Nation's capital and its members follow closely and participate in matters of local and national scope affecting the deaf.

The cry, "Where are the black deaf?" has been heard for a long time and we take pride in providing this newspaper as a vehicle for communication. With your help and encouragement we can keep in touch. Communication is a two-way street. This is our first issue, more will come. In the mean time subscribe, keep the faith, and let us hear from you, Today!

Linwood Smith
Editor, CCAD News

PRESIDENT'S MESSAGE

Writing for the first issue of our newsletter is kind of difficult since there is so much to relate and so little space to squeeze it into. Thus, in order to conserve energy(mine) and cover the whole spectrum of items simultaneously, I will simply insert the progress report I recently submitted to Mr. George Boyce, President and Mr. Sidney Taylor, Manager of Capital City Federal Savings and Loan Association, who contributed space for our present headquarters--

PROGRESS REPORT

The main objective of the Capital City Association of the Deaf is to promote the general welfare of the deaf in the Washington Metro Area. Although the CCAD has been in existence for several years as an association of black deaf persons in the D.C. area, it was only during the past two years that its membership solidified, reorganized and reshuffled its goals.

In the Fall of 1971, after over a year of inactivity except for sport events, CCAD members decided to broaden their goals. Monthly meetings were held, originally on Gallaudet College campus, later at the YMCA on 12th and T Streets-- both on the month to month basis. A housing committee was setup and the search began for a more permanent place to meet and socialize.

For a long time the black deaf in the Washington Metro Area lacked trained leadership and and opportunities for developing such, thus they were loosely organized and were unaware of the various services, jobs and training opportunities available. The new CCAD aim to change this with the influx of new and discovered leadership, and with the assistance of Deafpride, Inc. Through our close association with Deafpride we were better able to make community contacts which resulted in the acquisition of our present Center at 2010 Rhode Island Ave.,N.E. The space(1,383 sq.ft.) is being leased to CCAD at a very nominal rate by the Capital City Federal Savings and Loan Association, whose officials are very civic and community minded. The savings and loan association has assisted CCAD in various other ways also, such as donating chairs and a desk. This breakthrough enabled us to carry on our activities on a regular basis and gave more stability to the association.

Major Activities Sponsored by the Association: --

1. Athletics: Softball, basketball, and touch football teams
2. Holiday socials, of which the biggest is the Annual Memorial Day Dance which is attended by deaf persons from several other states. This year's social was held at La Gemma Banquet Hall and the Afterglow breakfast was held at CCAD Center.

Conversation Pieces

Tommy Williams, our former House Manager returned to sunny Florida. Tommy had trouble adjusting to the fickle DC weather and returned to Florida for health reasons. Best of luck to you Tommy! Write us often, We miss you!

Parents For Deaf Pride share CCAD Building

Every Sunday a group of parents of deaf children meet at the CCAD clubhouse to discuss current problems in Education of the deaf, learn Sign Language, and meet the adult deaf in Washington, these parents have virtually grown into our "Family" since many of them have joined CCAD and help us out in various activities. We are proud to share the building with them.

An old Chinese proverb: A good parent is worth 10,000 schoolmasters.

To obtain a list of facilities available for the special education of handicapped children in your area, write CLOSER LOOK, Box 1492, Washington, D.C. 20013.
To learn how to become a teacher of handicapped children, write to: CAREERS IN SPECIAL EDUCATION, Box 1492, Washington, D.C. 20013.

3. Get Acquainted Social: Representatives from organizations and agencies serving the deaf in the Washington metro area were invited to CCAD Center to: (1) provide members with the opportunity to become acquainted with the goals of other organizations of, for and/or serving the deaf in the area and (2) to help the community become aware of present and potential services offered by CCAD to deaf persons in the area and to parents of deaf and hard of hearing children. Representatives from 17 organizations were invited.

4. Weekly Captioned Films: Free captioned films are shown weekly to members at the Center.

5. "Ceremonies in Dark Old Men" Cast Party: The Hughes Theatre held their cast party at CCAD center following their first full length all black play. It was a mutual success.

6. Prior to remodeling their headquarters on the side adjoining CCAD, Parents for Deafpride held their regular Sunday afternoon meetings in CCAD's main meeting room and in turn CCAD used PDP's space during our large gatherings.

7. Beginning in September homemaker classes will be held on the monthly basis at the Center. The classes are planned and sponsored by Gallaudet College's Center for Continuing Education. More details regarding this will be published in the second issue of CCADNEWS.

Future and long-range plans include more community involvement, closer interaction with DEAFPRIDE, their parent group, MSSD students and deaf non-members within the community.

Membership in the association numbers approximately 45. The makeup is presently multiracial altho predominantly black. During special events and major activities which are open to non-members as well an average turnout of 120 is usually expected.

Incorporation papers and revised Bylaws are in the process of being completed.

Respectfully submitted,

Ernest E. Hairston
President

Although this report denotes some progress, we should be far from satisfied since there is so much more that could be done, so much more use that could be made of our Center, and so many more individuals that we could reach and help. LET'S ALL JOIN FORCES AND WORK TOWARD A COMMON GOAL.

Chess, anyone?

Several members of CCAD have been bitten by the Chess bug. Games are played each Friday night. Watch the bulletin board for announcement of the Chess tournament.

CCAD member has book published

International Books has recently announced the publication of _Silence, Love, And Kids I Know_, poems by Linwood Smith. Mr. Smith is a member of CCAD and the Educational Therapist at St. Elizabeths Hospital's Mental Health Program for the Deaf. Interested persons can order from

INTERNATIONAL BOOKS
P.O. BOX 6970
Washington, D.C. 20032

The price of the book is $3.95

The Project Committee is planning a trip for CCAD to Lancaster, Pa. during September. Lancaster, is famous as the "Home of the Amish". We will see how these live and learn of their culture. An interpreter will be provided. Also a side trip to the Amish farm village, Hershey Park, and other interesting places enroute is on the agenda. For information contact Helen Luckey or any member of the committee.

CCAD NEWS
P.O. BOX 7740
WASHINGTON, D.C.
20044

Philadelphia-Washington Ball
Early 1950's

After the Saturday Morning Meeting
Washington, D.C., 1949

Thanksgiving Dance, November 1949
Philadelphia Club for the Deaf

Philadelphia and Washington Silents Club Get-Together
May Dance, May 30, 1947

44

Washington Silents Society Bowling Club, 1950
Childress Collection

45

Officers, Philadelphia Club, 1951

Deaf Congregation Outside Church
Baltimore, Maryland, 1951

The Conference:
A Model

Often a point of view or focus point can shed a different light on the way things really are. For example, a Black deaf gathering—as mentioned earlier—was viewed as a place where Black deaf people congregated to drink, dance, or just get together to discuss a few things like forming sports teams. There are some exceptions, such as meetings of Black Deaf Advocates, a coalition of organizations and individuals advocating Black deaf citizens and their rights.

The First Black Deaf Conference held at Howard University on June 25-26, 1981, marked an important milestone and provided a model for others to emulate. Up to that time there were speculations that Black deaf people will not gather for anything other than socials and sports. This myth was laid to rest.

Objectives of the conference were as follows:

1. to better inform ourselves and the community about being both Black and deaf in America;

2. to identify and examine the social, economical, educational, religious, political, and health issues and their impact on the Black deaf community;

3. to formulate some strategies and problem solving techniques that participants can take back to their communities and use.

Workshops held over the two days involved six major areas: Education, Family, Social Services, Health and Mental Health, Employment, and Interpreting. A recurring statement at the conference was the need for Black people to work with Black people, in most instances because of the need for empathy, roots, role models, and special understanding, especially in the areas of mental health and social services.

Many speculations can be made regarding this conference. Individual registrants and guests may have their own interpretation. However, the conference served to demonstrate among other things that, contrary to popular belief, Black deaf people can and will plan for, conduct, and participate in functions other than those purely athletic or social in nature. Most significantly, a model has been established for future forums.

The Black deaf leaders and advocates from Cleveland, Ohio, agreed to continue the trend and hold a national conference the following year. In August

1982, Cleveland Chapter 2 of Black Deaf Advocates held a national conference and attracted nearly 300 participants.

Seven major issues were addressed at the Cleveland conference: mental health, education, Section 504, drugs and substance abuse, National Captioning Institute, hearing parents with deaf children, and social services.

More significantly, an executive secretary was elected to coordinate our national effort. This national push is to encourage more Black deaf persons to assume leadership roles, to become more active and visible, and to train potential Black deaf leaders.

Interesting enough, all this has caused anxiety among the general deaf leadership and raised such questions as, 'Why doesn't Black Deaf Advocates join the National Association of the Deaf?' and 'Does BDA compete with NAD for Black deaf members?' Similar questions were asked years ago, i.e. 'Why doesn't CCAD join MWAD?', etc. If we really analyze the questions and view the situation, we would realize that the questions were apparently blurted from the mouth before the mind had a chance to go into gear. First of all, BDA is wholly different from the NAD in structure, organization, and purpose. The basic goals, though, are similar—so are those of and for other organizations of and for the deaf. Secondly, any Black deaf individual, whether or not a member of BDA or CCAD and similar organizations, is free to also become a member of the NAD. Thirdly, these questions were not asked of the International Catholic Deaf Association (ICDA), the National Congress of Jewish Deaf (NCJD), and the Deaf Teletypewriters of Greater Washington (DTGW). If members of those organizations merit having their own identity without question or suspicion, why not the Black deaf?

This, we believe, is unconscious prejudice. One tends to fear the unknown and to be suspicious of things different from his/her own. One tends to prejudge rather than to venture an unbiased judgment. That is precisely where prejudice grows—from prejudgment. Now, let us view the situation under a different light. The major goal of BDA is to prepare Black deaf people for leadership roles—to train them in the art of planning, organizing, and implementing programs and goals—and to provide them with the opportunity to function as leaders or to interact with role models. This in turn would provide Black deaf leaders and potential leaders with the experience and confidence to interact with officials of the NAD and its membership. Otherwise, it would be the same old story—token Black person joins the organization and is a good old fellow, outmaneuvered by sophisticated white members, smiling all the while. It is time for a different approach. It is past the time for a change. This is the time for Black deaf people to pick up and wave their own flag and to feel good about themselves. One young participant at the Cleveland BDA Conference reflected the mood when she remarked, "I'm feeling so good about all this, I'm gonna cry." That is what it is all about—feeling good, crying out, and sharing it.

Self-esteem! Pride! Self-confidence! Conferences like those held by BDA encourage these virtures as well as the opportunity for personal growth and leadership training. They also give Black deaf people the satisfaction of having accomplished something "all by ourselves."

Some Highlights

Chuck Williams, chairman and leader of the Cleveland Chapter of BDA, leading a discussion on Section 504 of the Civil Rights Act.

Sandi LaRue, a Black deaf social worker, leading discussions on issues evolving around being both Black and deaf in America today and how this affects the psychosocial development of a person.

49

William Ortiga, Black hearing impaired social worker and mental health professional, providing information regarding types of services available to persons with mental health problems. One discussion involved factors causing mental health problems and the importance of race in counselling and in working with certain patients.

An entertainment break during the BDA Conference.

Glenn Anderson, the first Black deaf person to earn a Ph.D degree, discussing Black awareness and the need for organized visibility of Black deaf people.

Audience participation at the Washington BDA Conference.

Shirley Johnson, well known Black interpreter and founder of Bridges, interprets for Mayor Barry who gave the welcome address at the BDA Conference at Howard University in Washington, D.C.

Program Chairman, Linwood Smith, beaming with pleasure.

52

Lottie Crook (right), Chairperson of the Conference, elaborating on the award to Bob Howard, trainer and consultant.

Willard Shorter opening the Conference with an invocation.

Black Signs:
Whatever Happened to the Sign for "CORNBREAD"

Is there a Black sign language?

Do Black people sign differently from white people?

Why can't Black deaf people understand my signs?

These are questions we often hear. To those of us who have acquired the sign vocabulary used by the white majority, we often are subjected to the remark indicative of paternalistic largesse—"I don't want to hurt your feelings and I don't know how to say this, but you are the first Black deaf person whose signs I can understand."

To the first question, our answer is usually preceded by a smile and a polite "No." We maintain that there is no Black sign language. There is, however, a Black way of signing used by Black deaf people in their own cultural milieu—among families and friends, in social gatherings, and in deaf clubs. There are also sign vocabularies peculiar to the region where the Black deaf person came from, i.e. Black signs for cotton, tobacco, whites, tractor, cornbread, biscuits, and peanuts. These signs are still extensively used, in addition to approximately eight different signs for the word "bathroom." It should be pointed out that these signs are not just a regional variation. Many Southern white people do not use the same signs or do not know the signs used by their Black peers. These sign vocabularies may be classified as more or less indigenous to the Southern Black deaf populace.

Dr. James Woodward, a sociolinguist and well known authority on sign languages, published a perceptive study of Black signs. Dr. Woodward focused mainly on signs used by Black deaf children and adults in Georgia. He described variations in grammar, lexical variation, phonological variation, and variations in hand positions.

Historically, the roots of Black sign language developed because of societal attitudes and educational policy, especially in Southern schools for the deaf where dual systems had existed. Southern Black people from Georgia, North Carolina, South Carolina, Florida, Alabama, and Virginia used signs that were common to their respective schools.

As Black deaf people migrated from the South, they found that many of their signs were not widely used or known except among other Southern Black deaf persons who used them or had been exposed to them. Their signs tend to be either more colorful and demonstrative with nonverbal expressions and body language, or shortcut versions of standard signs. For example, the sign for a fancy car (Cadillac) would be formed with two "C" hands meeting and moving apart to form an elongated figure, while the whole upperbody is moving and the cheeks are puffed out. On the other hand, the sign for "mother" is simply formed by the "five" hand shape on the chin and the loose fingers wiggling.

As Black schools for the deaf merged with predominantly white schools, Black children began to sign "white," or as some others would say, "the Gallaudet way." This was more a survival than a social adaptation. Most adopted this way of signing to better themselves and to succeed in their new schools and so as not to appear different. However, among themselves, they retained their signed dialect and signed Black.

As a result, in the newly integrated schools or during cultural events, the sign "cornbread" was rarely used, if at all. Today, one rarely sees it, except when occasionally signed by older deaf persons at Black deaf clubs. In fact, it is rarely seen in any of the recent sign language books. The sign for "cornbread" is made by placing the hands in the praying position and rocking them from side to side. Its apparent death underscores the need to preserve this part of Black deaf culture. It has been said that when one destroys a people's language, one destroys a people. The future of Black signs does not seem promising. As new generations emerge, legacies of the past are forgotten. Today, there seems to be a cultural erosion and a need to preserve the traditions, beliefs, language, and ideals of Black deaf people.

There is no Black sign language, but Black deaf people are proud to communicate in their own special way, using their own special signs.

Common Bonds and Stepping Stones

Hundreds of Black deaf children have never had the opportunity to talk with or meet Black deaf adults during their formative years. They undergo the challenge of having to get along in a hearing environment without role models who can ease their adjustment, give them pride, encouragement, and offer a few tricks of the trade on "getting through."

Eventually, many of them do adjust. However, in our experience we have seen many in need of emotional, psychological, and psychiatric help which could have been avoided had they met others who have gone down the same path and who could have provided a helping hand and served as stepping stones.

Each of the contributors to this section brings a variety of experiences to the field of deafness and in working for the advancement of deaf people on a local, national, or international level. They range from a housewife with six children in New York City to the founder of more than four schools for the deaf serving hundreds in Africa. From a former electronics worker to a member of the Gallaudet College Board of Trustees.

From listening to each of them, one gains a better perspective of what it is like to be a member of a double minority. They share their joys, frustrations, dreams, fears, struggles, and hopes. One learns of roots and common bonds that tie many of them together despite age, background, achievements, and goals. One learns of family . . . of friends . . . of love . . . of life.

Shirley Allen

Shirley Allen was born in Tyler, Texas. She attended public schools in Texas and, in 1959, entered Talladega College in Alabama to major in Music. At 20 years old, she became deaf from the use of streptomycin. She enrolled at Gallaudet College in Washington, D.C. in 1963 and graduated with a B.A. in English. In 1972, she earned her M.A. degree in Guidance and Counseling from Howard University. She has worked for the Peace Corps, taught and counseled at Gallaudet College, and is now an Assistant Professor of Developmental Education at the National Technical Institute for the Deaf. An accomplished actress, she has appeared in numerous stage productions, among which are *The American Dream* and *Ceremonies In Dark Old Men* at Gallaudet.

Shirley, you are one of those people who became deaf late in life, at age 20. What was your early education like? And how did deafness affect you?

Since I lost my hearing at 20, I went to public schools. I was a leader throughout grade and high school. I was majoring in Music with emphasis on Piano and Education in college. I lost my hearing from the use of streptomycin. After staying out of school for a year because of illness, I returned after losing my hearing and finished my requirements for Music. I transferred to Gallaudet in 1963 and majored in Sociology and English. I graduated in 1966 and received my M.A. in Guidance and Counseling from Howard University in 1972.

How were Black students from the hearing colleges you attended different from those at Gallaudet?

Black students at hearing colleges were not much different from those at schools for the deaf. There was quite a bit more awareness of the "Black problem," but that's a majority problem and the deaf Blacks must cope with a majority of minority problems, get it? At Gallaudet, there were not enough Blacks to have a feeling of comradeship, brotherhood—that kind of thing. Most of the Blacks came from Black schools and acted in *awe* of the institution instead of trying to ask questions on where the place was at, where it was going, and why there weren't more Blacks!

How did you hear about Gallaudet?

A friend of my aunt in Texas has a deaf nephew, and when she found out that I had become deaf, she mentioned him. He was a student at Gallaudet at that time.

It must have been very traumatic to change your plans from a career in music at 20. What did the realization that you were deaf do to your outlook on life?

My becoming deaf was one of the most important events that ever happened to me. It changed my whole attitude about life. I had open plans for years to be a music teacher and secret plans of being a blues singer. I practiced piano blindfolded for years just in case I went blind. It never occurred to me that I could or would become deaf. I do not feel, prior to my deafness, that I had any feelings one way or the other about so-called handicapped people. I've become more sensitive, concerned about, and loving towards others. This is great in that all the time you feel yourself giving, you feel yourself receiving also.

Now that your plans have changed, where are you heading?

I was majoring in Music Education and it is hard to imagine how one can put emphasis on music most of his life and become an assistant professor in Developmental Education for the deaf. However, a basic feeling of real love for people in general and the "push to be somebody" would evidently lead to working with people on a professional basis.

How did you adjust to losing your hearing at such a late stage in your life?

Many have asked how I "coped" or adjusted with losing my hearing so late in life. I feel I've coped, but not adjusted. In fact, to me, most people (hearing or deaf) with whom I come into contact do not seem adjusted. My majors in school were Music, Sociology, English (B.A.), and Counselling (M.A.), so with such a diverse background it is hard to say where I am going. My great love for students (particularly college students) will more than likely keep me in the field of education and in a role where I will be in direct contact on a daily basis with them.

We're very much concerned with the areas of self-esteem and pride for Black deaf youth. What can you say in order to encourage young deaf persons who might be feeling that life has nothing to offer them simply because of the fact that they cannot hear?

Know yourself. Feel that you will live forever and have plenty of time to learn about yourself. Work as if you will die tomorrow so that you will feel accomplishments and worthiness. Give your best in whatever you feel like giving and while you are raising the fist of power, look to God and be thankful. Make love a meaningful experience. No matter how many times you get discouraged, keep the humor in your life and in the lives of others around you. Learn to give without expecting something in return and you will always encounter little surprises. Set achievable goals and stick with them. Don't look at failure as a destroyer, but rather as a helping hand that is pushing you forward. Think positive, although it is the hardest job around today!

Katie Brown

Katie Brown is currently a counselor at the Jewish Vocational Service Agency in Chicago, Illinois. She has worked as a parish worker, workshop supervisor, and psychometrist. She received her B.A. degree from Gallaudet College in 1964 and her M.A. degree from DePaul University in Chicago.

Mrs. Brown is affiliated with the National Rehabilitation Association and the Professional Rehabilitation Workers with the Adult Deaf. She has served on the National Advisory Group of the National Technical Institute for the Deaf and on the Gallaudet College Board of Trustees.

Katie, we would like to begin by asking you when you became deaf and how it affected your education?

I had reached the fifth grade in the public schools of St. Louis, Missouri, before I lost my hearing. Afterwards, I attended the Charles Henry Turner School for the Handicapped.

You attended Gallaudet while you had a family in Chicago. Could you tell us how you managed to succeed and complete your education while supporting your family?

I did not have to support my family. My husband did that. Because my husband had to keep things going for himself and my boys at home, money was in short supply for me. I usually had some kind of job around campus and I got a few awards, scholarships, and grants-in-aid. At that time, the Vocational Rehabilitation Division would not support a housewife. Later on, DVR did pay some of my fees, but money for my personal expenses was always a problem. What motivated me was the knowledge that I was not getting any younger and I'd never get another chance like that. I had been a nonprofessional helper to the deaf for many years and here was a chance to get "know-how" to enable me to be a better helper.

After you graduated from high school, what were your vocational aspirations? Was there any reason why you did not go to college earlier?

When I graduated from high school, that was *it*. I think I was the only person in my family to ever do that and college never crossed my mind. What's more, I married a year before I finished high school. I had never heard of Gallaudet. I know now that smart white kids were prepared for Gallaudet, but for poor Blacks at that time, it was "not yet." I wouldn't have believed that a Black deaf person could go to college if you had told me and since no one did tell me, I never gave it a thought.

How did you begin working with the deaf?

A talk with a Lutheran minister during which he suggested that if I had more talent or a better understanding of what went on about me, it was God's wish that I share and use it for those who had need of it. The change did not come overnight, but I began to feel more humble and, as I matured, I stopped looking down on the deaf who were not like me. I began to associate with them wholeheartedly and made myself available, not condescendingly but as one of them. They responded by seeking me out and the forefinger applied with a push under the nose was used less and less against me. After marriage, two sons, and many years of trying to be of service to the deaf, the turning point came when I was trying to help one of my husband's friends obtain employment. The man had lost the job that he held for 30 years. He'd had me writing letters to different places asking for employment. None of them were answered. Then I remembered that my husband had gotten his job through the Division of Vocational Rehabilitation, so I decided to send him there. The letter I wrote to state his case and introduce him to the DVR was the pivot point. The counselor who read the letter asked my friend if the writer was deaf and I was on my way to Gallaudet nine months later.

Did your degree make it any easier for you to get a job?

Well, first of all, a B.A. degree in Sociology is not enough to get a good professional job in Chicago if a deaf person cannot hear well enough to use the telephone. A new program was being planned for the deaf, however, and my vocational rehabilitation counselor who kept abreast of such things suggested that I go for an M.A. degree in psychology so that I could have opportunities to work with the new program. This new program was the Community Project for the Deaf at Chicago Jewish Vocational Services.

What kind of work are you doing now?

For the past six years, most of my work has been with the deaf of minimal language skills. As a Vocational Counselor, I counsel, guide, and teach. I try to spark motivation, a desire for independence, and everything I know to help my clients become self-supporting, happy members of the community.

What problems have you come across thus far?

I have found in my work with the deaf of minimal language skills that they are often unloved and unwanted. And it seems that the majority are either over-protected or neglected. Too few of them come well adjusted and eager to take their place in society as contributing members. I have also found that it is difficult to find foster homes for them. Those homes and institutions that exist to help needy children are very reluctant to take deaf children, which may be the reason we find so many deaf children in mental institutions.

Albert Rhodes worked at Flanner House, a home for deaf men in Indianapolis, Indiana. He said that you were instrumental in helping him with this project. Do you foresee this happening in Chicago?

Yes! That's my aspiration, to have a home for these Black youngsters where they can find love, understanding, and support to help them become the self-sustaining human beings they were meant to be.

As a professional worker with the deaf, do you see any specific needs for young deaf people?

The need of all young deaf people NOW is education and this is even more important for young Black people. If you do not have academic ability, learn a trade. But the most important thing for the deaf to learn is to accept their limitations and make the most of their assets. Be realistic, if all you can do is mop floors, be the best floor mopper there is. Please don't spend any of your energy being jealous of your friend who works in an office. As simple as you may think your job is, it might (but shouldn't) surprise you to find out that your office friend could not do it half as well. All of us have talent for something special and they are not at all similar, so be happy with the job you have, polish it, and perfect it. If you learn to accept your limitations and make the most of your assets, you can lead happier productive lives. Our mental institutions are full of people who could not accept what they could not change.

Mary Cheese

Mary Cheese is the mother of six children. She resides in New York City. From four to five years old, she was blind, and at 13 lost her hearing. Mrs. Cheese attended the day school for the deaf at Junior High School 47 in New York and is very active in church and social affairs. She was the first woman president of the Imperials Club for the Deaf. Although not a college graduate, Mrs. Cheese serves as a sort of "Mother Superior" to many Black deaf youth and adults.

Mary, we have heard that you once were blind. Could you comment on this a little?

I was blind from four to five years old. I did not enter public school until I was seven. My mother died when I was two and I was raised by my two married sisters. I was taken from one eye clinic to another and finally my stepmother found a doctor who could help me. Since I had normal hearing and speech, my stepmother was able to train me at home. At seven, I went to the first grade.

How did you happen to regain your eyesight?

An eye operation to remove a cataract was performed at Columbia Presbyterian Hospital. I was not born blind, but became blind at the age of four and remained so for the entire year. Eye drops were able to help me at that time.

How did you become deaf?

When I was 13, some friends and I were riding bicycles when suddenly I was struck by a truck and spent months in the hospital. Little by little my hearing decreased. I entered the Lexington School for the Deaf, but stayed for less than a month. I then went to Junior High School 47 and stayed until the ninth grade.

Any thoughts about that?

After marriage and six children, I've constantly regretted dropping out of school before graduation and feel the need for more education, but at that time there was no way I could manage to enter high school. Too many conflicts and raising the children kept me busy. Still I was able to keep up with my reading and my dictionary was a valuable guide with difficult words. As the children grew older, I was able to travel, join clubs, and become more active in church and deaf affairs. The thirst for higher learning has not diminished but somehow I feel unable to reach my goal.

What is your goal?

I'm very busy at church and I sing in the choir. I am very much interested in helping people and I would like to register for a high school education and from there go on to college and enter the field of social work.

What do you hope to accomplish as the first female president of the Imperials Club for the Deaf?

My first goal is to see that the club gets a clubhouse. Also an office with an experienced social worker who can help the deaf with various problems. I would also like to start a back-to-school program for those who have never had a chance to finish. Then make every member of the club a voter. Many Black deaf people have never voted and do not understand why they should.

What has encouraged you to become interested in social work?

I am really interested in nursing, and if it wasn't for my hearing loss, I would probably be a nurse now. But social work interests me because the Black deaf bring so many of their problems to me to solve and sometimes I find I do not have the experience to help them with certain problems and have to seek an agency that can help them.

Tell us about some of the problems of Black deaf people in New York City and what you feel needs to be done.

I'm very worried and concerned about Black deaf people in New York. Not only with adults but children as well. Black deaf adults here for the most part are bitter. They feel that society has forgotten them. That they are "lost" people. In a way this is true. There are no agencies or connections concerned with the Black deaf. It is as if they don't exist. Much is needed to help these people, a complete program—job training, health and welfare office to counsel, schooling, and help for the elderly Black person and many others. The younger deaf still in school need Total Communication. Many of them do not know sign language since there is so much emphasis on learning how to talk at the expense of learning language. Language includes reading and writing which is important for advancement. This lack of good language ability is what hurts and restricts so many of the Black deaf who are victims of poor school programs that believe the "hearing" way or the "white" way are the only ways of doing things. Those who drop out are often the type hearing people refer to as "deaf and dumb." These teenagers lack good educational background and their writing is often scrambled. They are not job material and need not only training in a trade but more schooling as well.

Then, too, teenage girls have little understanding of birth control, venereal disease, and other body germs. I feel that every parent of deaf children should be given a leaflet or handbook concerning the needs of these children. Some schools do not teach this kind of hygiene. White deaf girls learn from concerned parents. Many Black hearing parents, who are victims of our society, are overburdened with the social and economic problems affecting Black people. As a result, they have little time and energy to be of help to their deaf children who need much more help than hearing children do. I believe it is up to those Black deaf adults who understand these problems to provide leadership and guidance to improve the well-being of Black deaf people.

Do you have any specific advice you would pass along to young girls?

First, I would tell young girls to "stay in school." Marriage and early employment aren't that important in the early years. The lack of a complete education can make you feel empty inside. Black deaf people, especially women, can find brighter future rewards by remaining on the educational bandwagon. No one is ever too old to learn. Age really means nothing. If you want an education, set about getting one and work hard to reach your goals, then you can proudly say, "My hearing loss is no handicap . . . I am as good as anyone else."

Albert Couthen

Al Couthen graduated from the American School for the Deaf in 1961 and from Gallaudet College in 1966. He returned to A.S.D. and worked as a dormitory counselor, head coach of football and track, health and safety instructor, and Dean of Boys. He attended the National Leadership Training Program at California State University, Northridge, in 1975 and was awarded a Master of Arts Degree in Educational Administration and Supervision. For the next two years, he was Director of Counseling Services in the Connecticut State Commission of the Deaf and Hearing Impaired. From 1977, he served as physical education instructor and After School Program Coordinator at the Kendall Demonstration Elementary School. He is presently assistant principal at KDES.

Al, tell us about your school years at the American School for the Deaf.

The years I spent at the American School for the Deaf were very rewarding. I would like to mention two areas which provided me excellent learning experience. First, the academic program at ASD. During my days at ASD, there were several good teachers who encouraged me to excel in my studies. Ms. Ethel Giett was one who always emphasized to me that academic work is very important for my career. She always showed me her concerns about my school work and always reminded me that the academic is first and the athletic is second. Secondly, the athletic program at ASD. Mr. Oscar Shirley, who was my favorite coach, always emphasized to me that the successful athlete has to develop himself and work very hard to improve his skills. He always told me various sports stories and about his athletic days. He was the person who encouraged me to choose Physical Education and coaching as my career. I feel that these two people were largely responsible for my present career.

What do you feel was the main thing that contributed to your success?

I would say that my ability to work with different people contributed to my success. It has been my experience to learn from trial and error and try to do my best the next time. It is a challenge to be a leader. I am willing to listen to people's ideas and be able to make a decision.

You were one of Gallaudet's finest athletes, what do you see as the place of sports in Black deaf adolescents?

I know that Black deaf adolescents want to be excellent athletes. I feel that they should have the opportunity to participate, but I think that they should be aware that the academic program is very important to their career. They should be taught that academic subjects come first and sports come second. The sports field is a good avenue for Black deaf adolescents, but it is very important that they know and understand that their careers depend on their success in academics.

What does your present position involve? What do you do?

My present position is Assistant Principal at Kendall Demonstration Elementary School in Washington, D.C. My responsibilities are supervisor for Art, Physical Education, Home Economics, and the Music Department. I am also in charge of the Transportation Service, Food Services, After School Programs, and the Volunteer Program.

What are some of the concerns you hear from parents of Black deaf children in the elementary department?

I would like to reverse this question. I think that the parents of Black students need Parent Education on Deafness. I feel that this would help them to understand deafness and to have better and realistic expectations from their Black deaf child(ren). If the Black parents can communicate with their deaf child(ren) by using sign language and get involved in deaf community activities and school activities, I feel that this will contribute to a better family life for the child(ren). I feel that sign language communication should be used in the home environment at all times.

What are your future goals?

To be very honest, as of now I don't expect that I am going to go that far as Assistant Principal. However, I would like to be head of a deaf school or a director of a national organization for the deaf. Right now, I am very involved with my present jobs and the various community activities.

Dr. Andrew Foster

Andrew Foster was the first Black person to graduate from Gallaudet College. He became deaf at 11 and attended the Alabama School for the Deaf. At 17, he moved to Detroit, Michigan, and since he was a minor and his parents lived in another state, he was denied admission to the Michigan State School for the Deaf. Andrew took a factory job and high school courses by correspondence, while attending the Detroit Institute of Commerce at night.

After gaining his high school diploma, he entered Gallaudet College and completed work for his B.A. in three years by taking summer courses at Hampton Institute. He earned a M.A. degree from Eastern Michigan University and a B.A. in Missions from Seattle Pacific College. In 1956, he founded the Christian Mission for Deaf Africans and, in 1957, journeyed to West Africa to begin his missionary work with the deaf. He has pioneered educational and gospel work in Ghana, Nigeria, and indirectly in Liberia. In recognition of his unique accomplishments and service, Gallaudet College conferred upon him a Doctor of Humane Letters degree.

Dr. Foster, your story should be one of utmost importance to all of us. As the first Black graduate of Gallaudet College, we want to begin by asking about your deafness.

When I was 11 years old, I was stricken by spinal meningitis. Upon recovery, the disease left no crippling defect, but the high fever from the disease and medication completely destroyed the nerves of my hearing and I became profoundly deaf. My brother was stricken too.

Since there is more than one family member who is deaf, what was your adjustment like?

My brother and I adjusted to our deafness very well. We resumed our playing with the neighborhood kids at camp and Sunday school. I spent almost five years at the Alabama School for the Deaf in Talladega. I often wondered how a deaf person could get ahead in life and education being what it was in the South then, I set out for Detroit on my own at 17. In Detroit, one of my first objectives was to find a church for the deaf. Their meeting place turned out to be a small, old brick house where the minister lived upstairs and the downstairs walls had been moved to make an assembly room. A front section of the hall was reserved for the deaf. Several persons interpreted and the deaf were always mentioned publicly and in prayer by the minister, B. M. Nottage. But my greatest impact came on Sunday afternoons when the entire hall was used for deaf people. Walter J. Lyon worked with us for about 45 years. He was truly an inspiration to me. Brother Nottage and Brother *Lion,* as he was affectionately called, gave me my impetus to become a minister.

Your educational background is noteworthy, could we back up a little and have you tell us how you completed Gallaudet in three years?

I received a full four-year Congressional scholarship to Gallaudet College and, by taking summer sessions at Hampton Institute, I got my B.A. degree in Education in three years. In June 1954, I received my M.A. degree in Education from Michigan State Normal College (now Eastern Michigan University) at Ypsilanti. In 1956, I completed studies for the missionary at Seattle Pacific College.

In 1956, you founded the Christian Mission for Deaf Africans, what was that?

In 1956, the Christian Mission for Deaf Africans was incorporated in Michigan with its office in Detroit. This ministry, which operated with a general council and advisory board, exists to promote the spiritual and educational welfare of the deaf in Africa.

What do you hope in this regard?

The immediate task is twofold: We hope to move people and teach them about the Bible. We aim to use boarding, primary, and vocational schools where the Bible forms part of the curriculum. Also Sunday schools, Bible classes, camps, and training Christian leaders are also part of our plans. We have established schools in Nigeria, Ghana, and the Ivory Coast. The school in Ghana has 139 students plus about 800 on the waiting list. Deaf since birth or infancy, many of the students had known no language or even words. Many parents conceal them out of shame. Some were made to spend their days working on farms, while the more able brothers and sisters were sent to school. A few tried to adapt to society; others, understandably, withdrew themselves. More unfortunately, their spiritual darkness was great too. The cruel double handicap of deafness and illiteracy largely shuts out the Gospel of Jesus Christ. To penetrate these barriers for a regular ministry, special schools for the deaf were necessary. None existed in West Africa prior to 1957.

How many deaf people are there in Africa?

No one knows for certain. However, a general idea might be obtained by viewing statistics in other countries. In America, one out of every 2,000 is deaf; in Italy one out of every 1,000; and in Ghana, one to every 1,000 persons.

Are you training leaders for the deaf in Africa?

Yes, training educational and spiritual leaders among the deaf has been a foremost objective since first arriving in West Africa in 1957. Both deaf and hearing persons have been advised, oriented, and, in some cases, assisted financially to train for such roles. Some of the "trainees" have studied at Gallaudet. Several have returned to Ghana and Nigeria and are capably assisting their governments with the social affairs of the deaf.

What do you foresee for the future?

That all depends, many factors must be considered. Education of the deaf is mushrooming. Roughly 500 deaf youths are now literate in West Africa; over twice that number are studying in various special schools. Elsewhere on the continent, around 50 schools for the deaf now exist with a staggering student and alumni population. Many countries as yet have no facilities for their deaf citizens (one out of every thousand persons) while others are begging for more! In Africa, we too have the problem of secularism, materialism, pornography, liberalism, religious sects, paganism, and so on. The future, therefore, depends upon our attitude today towards the Bible's formula for evangelizing the world, even deaf Africans. As we are aware, the Scripture's methods are earnest prayer, supporting biblically sound ministries, and personal service. To maintain and expand this gospel witness among the deaf of Africa, may God challenge each and every one of us like Joshua, "There remaineth yet very much land to be possessed." Tomorrow may be too late!

Thank you Dr. Foster for an inspiring and informative interview and may your work and example always be remembered.

Jeremiah Germany
1930–1977

Jeremiah Germany was a Vocational Counselor at the California School for the Deaf in Berkeley, California. He taught at the Florida School for the Deaf, the Tennessee School for the Deaf, the New Jersey School for the Deaf, and adult education classes in California. He obtained his B.A. degree from Gallaudet College in 1956 and his M.A. degree from California State University in 1973 where he was a member of the Leadership Training Program in the area of deafness.

Mr. Germany was one of the first Black students to be accepted at Gallaudet during the early 1950's.

Jerry, tell us something about your early educational experience.

I lost my hearing through spinal meningitis. I went to the Alabama School for the Negro Deaf at Talladega and started in the beginners program. During my eight years at Talladega, graduation was something unheard of in this separate program for Blacks and was only known to happen in the dual system reserved for whites. Afterwards, I moved to Detroit and later enrolled in the Michigan School for the Deaf at Flint. At the Michigan School for the Deaf, I was able to get some vocational training, participate in sports, and get a reasonable secondary education.

What are some significant events that contributed to your success?

While at the Alabama School, I was fortunate to have a deaf teacher who was very civic minded and with good insight into the learning problems of deaf students. This person happened to be white (Blacks were not hired as instructors at that school then) and very much dedicated to his teaching as were most of the teachers who were deaf as I now recall. This teacher had a very touching and dramatic way of arousing self-awareness in the students. This was a big factor in my later curiousity about myself as a Black person in the world and later interest in doing outside reading beyond that called for in class. While at the Michigan School for the Deaf, the great civil rights movement was just starting to take place. Jackie Robinson had just broken into major league baseball, the U.S. Supreme Court had ordered the University of Texas to admit its first Black student, and other sweeping changes were taking place in our government. Out of class I was reading just about every bit of news the civil rights movement made and felt a strong identification with it.

This was a factor in my eventually applying for admission to Gallaudet College which had no Black students in its program. My application was accepted, but I failed to pass the examination for admission for the obvious reason that the Michigan School was reluctant to be a party in pushing for integration at Gallaudet College. This was done by not placing me in the classes with the college bound students. However, after some protest and another try, I was fortunate to become the second Black student accepted at Gallaudet in the early 1950's.

After graduation from Gallaudet you had a wide and varied teaching career. Can you elaborate on this?

After obtaining my Bachelor's degree in Education from Gallaudet, I taught at the Florida School for the Deaf in St. Augustine, the Tennessee School for the Deaf in Knoxville, the New Jersey School for the Deaf in West Trenton, and now the California School for the Deaf at Berkeley. In the first two schools, I did some coaching, acted as a dormitory counselor, and advised several school clubs. My present position at the California School came by way of obtaining my Master's degree in Educational Administration from California State University, Northridge, in 1973. My long range goal is to become a coordinator of an educational or rehabilitation program for the deaf.

Jerry, in view of your experience, do you have any advice for young Black deaf people?

My advice to young Black deaf youth is to reach for the top. By that I mean strive for high goals in life. The best way to do that is to explore a few areas of occupational interests and preferences. Find out what the physical demands and work environment is like, then prepare yourself for the occupation of your preference.

Today, many of our young Black youth, both deaf and hearing, do not know what they want to do in life. Many try to bluff their way through the educational system, all of which is a great waste of human resources, time, and money. Even if you do not agree with our present system, try to learn as much about it by getting a thorough education. Then, as a mature adult, you'll be in a better position to work toward changes within the system.

Above all, know what your rights are as a citizen, as a deaf person, as a member of a minority group, as a disabled person, and your rights to an education and what available programs are open to you. Learn some saleable skills and know what you want and can do. Don't just say, I am going to get a job, and not have a saleable skill or not know what you want.

James Magness

James Magness was formerly a Career Development counselor at Gallaudet College. He was born in Lincolnton, North Carolina, and obtained his B.A. from Gallaudet College in 1955 and his M.A. from the State University of New York at Albany in 1971.

The father of four children, Mr. Magness has had an extensive teaching and coaching background. He has attended North Carolina A & T College, Florida State University, and the University of Kansas. He has taught and coached at the Florida School for the Deaf and the New York State School for the Deaf at Rome, New York. Mr. Magness served as President of the Capital City Club for the Deaf in Washington and as a lecturer in the Graduate School of Counseling and Placement at Gallaudet College. Mr. Magness retired from his position at Gallaudet in 1977 due to a disability; however, he is still active in church and is a deacon at Shiloh Baptist church in Washington.

Jim, let's begin by asking you when you lost your hearing?

I am one of those people who the experts say became deaf "later in life." I became deaf at 19. I attended public schools all my life in North Carolina, plus one year in a hearing college before I became deaf. My early educational experiences were typical of any other hearing person attending a hearing school. Two years of French were taken in high school and I am still able to speak, write, and read it due to the fact that at the time I could hear and the pronunciation of words was required. My two years of Spanish at Gallaudet only provided a good grade. Being on the football and baseball teams in high school was particularly satisfying to me, yet during my senior year I was hit on the head with a pitched ball which could possibly have caused my deafness one year later. However, there is no proof. Nothing really was exciting about my early educational experience as I had no aim to do anything upon the completion of high school but make a possible move "up north" where Blacks were "treated" better.

How did your deafness affect you?

I believe my deafness is the most significant contribution to my success. Had I been a hearing person, the competition would have been keener, I believe. Since I am Black, I feel that my deafness afforded me three years of a free education at Gallaudet which I could not afford had I been a hearing person. The fact that Black deaf persons were direly needed in schools for the deaf provided me with an opportunity to consider teaching as my future work.

The main event contributing to my success would be my education and the fact that I became deaf at the right time—after learning to talk, write, and read, knowing what the hearing world was all about.

Jim, your success as a teacher, counselor, and coach at the New York School for the Deaf in Rome leaves a remarkable impression on us. But now that that is behind you, what lies ahead?

My vocational aspiration is to obtain a degree in Administration as I want to be a principal or Superintendent in a school for the deaf, preferably a new one, where I would be able to start from scratch, to serve as a model and influence deaf youths to strive harder. I was able to advance to where I am now because of my coaching experience, great rapport with my students, and a feeling that all students, regardless of their color, intelligence, or handicap, were humans needing love and understanding. This attests to the fact that the school's yearbook was dedicated to me by a student body of 95 percent white students at Rome, New York. To top this off, I was the only Black person employed at the school in any capacity, the school did not even have a Black janitor or food service worker. That the students were allowed to decide who to dedicate their school yearbook to was a good demonstration in self-responsibility for the children. Had the adults at Rome been allowed to make the same decision, I doubt I would have received such an honor.

What would you advise young Black deaf persons in particular?

My advice to young Blacks is to refuse handouts (welfare, SSI, etc.) unless it is desperately needed. Any able-bodied man should want to and should work for his living as an accomplishment. Blacks must use other Blacks as models, motivate themselves to be or try to be the same or better, and work hard to meet this goal. It is easy to tell what kind of mind a person has by the conversations he conducts. Does he talk about people, ideas, or events? I would suggest that young Blacks keep themselves abreast of happenings in the world and that this awareness of world happenings is possibly the only solution to their problems of underemployment, undereducation, and "under" everything else.

Black deaf youth need to believe that as individuals they are as good or better than any other man on this earth. When they have the feeling of being somebody, somebody with dignity, self-respect, and pride, then and only then can they meet the challenges the world puts before them.

I would advise them not to be tools, something that others use. We love people and use tools. To clarify this, I would encourage them to spend more time hitting the books instead of spending all their time hitting the opposing lineman, hitting the nets, hitting a baseball over the fence, or even yet beating up his Black brother in a boxing match. Carrying a football, shooting a basketball, or hitting a baseball is not the only way to succeed in life. Education is not the only way either, but an education stays with us longer than sports ability and opens up more opportunities. So instead of merely aspiring to be great athletes, Black deaf youth should strive to become great scholars. The same comments can be applied to girls who aspire to be housewives. It is no longer necessary for a woman to waste her talents because of the old-fashioned belief that her place is in the home.

Carolyn McCaskill

Carolyn McCaskill is a counseling student at Gallaudet College. During the annual Gallaudet College Pageant in 1976, she was crowned Miss Gallaudet. She is an accomplished stage performer who received recognition during the Miss Gallaudet Pageant for singing "Where Are You Going To?" from the movie, *Mahogany*. As a Psychology major, she aspires to be a social worker or counselor and at the same time continue performing with theater groups.

Carolyn, how and when did you become deaf?

I became deaf at the age of five. My mother noticed that my sister and I were not responding quickly to her. She took us to several doctors who recommended that we have our tonsils removed. Unfortunately, having our tonsils removed did not help us. My hearing loss is due to either nerve deafness or is hereditary. I have a deaf sister, a deaf cousin, and an uncle who is hard-of-hearing.

What were your early years like?

My education began at a public school in Mobile. I did not attend any preschool or kindergarten. However, I remained in public school from the first to the eighth grade. I found it very frustrating that I was not in a program for the deaf. Somehow I convinced my mother to allow me and my sister to transfer to the Alabama School for the Deaf. The school played a big part in my life because I felt more sure of myself and was in a different educational environment where I learned sign language and met other deaf people. Later I took the entrance examination to Gallaudet and was accepted for admission. My sister was also admitted. I noticed that the Black deaf who left school always ended up getting a job in a factory, working with machines or as a maid, and I said to myself, "No way I'm going to do that, no way." I knew that some of them had the qualifications to do better than that, but they went along with the others, saying that Blacks are dumb, that they can't learn. I decided I was going to have to work harder than anyone else.

What encouraged you to enter the Miss Gallaudet Pageant?

I decided to enter the Pageant through the persuasion of my friends. I really had no idea or thought of entering. After being selected first runner-up in 1974, I felt as if I was in a dream. The whole thing was so beautiful.

My decision to try again was basically because of the fun I had becoming acquainted with new people and also representing the Ebony Harambee Club, a new club recently established at Gallaudet College. One of my friends, Betty Saddler of Chicago, was a real help in getting and keeping me psyched up for the Pageant.

In 1975, you won the Pageant. What was your reaction?

I was shocked! It was almost unbelievable! I felt as if I were really dreaming. It was a moment I'll always remember and a moment I love to share with others. I was very happy.

How would you apply what you have learned to help deaf women in the future?

I would like to be a social worker or counselor and through that help others. Hopefully, when I graduate I will be in a position to draw from my experiences at Gallaudet, people I've met, the honor of being Miss Gallaudet, and all of the other wonderful things that have happened to me, and accomplish my goals.

Can you comment specifically on the status of Black deaf women on the college level?

First, you notice the numbers. If you look around you note that there are a larger number of Black deaf people in college programs than in previous years. Women have more choices in finding good jobs, but I have noticed that while many of us are in college we have trouble coping with a new environment that has less Blacks than our state school for the deaf. At Gallaudet, the Ebony Harambee Club has provided us with a psychosocial base to succeed. I hope that club continues.

Albert Rhodes

Albert "Tubby" Rhodes graduated from the Indiana School for the Deaf. Mr. Rhodes was formerly a counselor with the Crossroads Rehabilitation program in Indianapolis and the former Director of Flanner House, a halfway house for the deaf in Indianapolis, Indiana.

Mr. Rhodes has worked for over 32 years in volunteer community services and para-professional positions with deaf organizations and agencies. He has been employed by the P. R. Mallory Electronics company for over 30 years.

Mr. Rhodes was one of the founders of Black deaf clubs, such as the Lincoln Club for the Deaf in Chicago and the Cleveland Silent Club in Cleveland, Ohio. He also served as president of the Greater Indianapolis Club for the Deaf. Since 1971, he has been working to set up Adult Basic Education programs in Indiana, a direct result of the training and experience he gained as a participant in Project DAWN at California State University, Northridge.

Tubby, you attended and graduated from the Indiana School for the Deaf and afterwards went to public school. What were some of the experiences you remember most?

I was 17 years old when I enrolled in Crispus Attucks High School in Indiana. I graduated when I was 21. It was a new experience being in a predominantly Black high school. The principal of Attucks high school eased my adjustment to the school by informing all of the teachers that I was deaf and, with some awareness of my hearing problem, I would be able to participate in their classes. I am thankful to the principal, Mr. Coleman, who had lots of faith in me and believed I had the ability and courage to make it.

The first day of class I had to take the first row so I could read the teacher's lips. Interpreters, as we know them today, did not exist at that time. The students were very cooperative. They really thought I needed a lot of help if I could not hear the teacher. Mr. Walker, my first teacher, had very good mouth movements that were easy to read. Sometimes he'd look sideways and talk or turn around facing the blackboard. That gave me a hard time. I knew I missed a lot, but some of my fellow students near me wrote notes to help me with class lectures.

I recall the many friends I made in high school, especially one student, Bob Williams, who had wanted to learn how to communicate with me. He became very fluent in fingerspelling within a short time. He could also do some sign language. We graduated together. He went to the University of Indiana, but I did not go along with him and I have regretted it. He is now a physician at the Health Center Hospital in Indianapolis.

We are aware of many educational barriers to deaf Blacks when you were growing up. Did you ever apply for college?

The reason I did not go to Gallaudet College was because, prior to 1949, educational programs were segregated in Washington, including Gallaudet College. I was informed in my sophomore year at the Indiana School for the Deaf that Blacks were not allowed to go to Gallaudet. Four of us Black students did not know what to do after we learned this. Naturally, I lost interest in studying with no goals to aim for. Going to Gallaudet was my primary goal since many graduates of the Indiana school went there. My other goal was to play professional football. I played semi-pro football for four years. I quit when I was not selected to attend a professional training camp, but I have never regretted that I tried out.

You have worked at Crossroads Rehabilitation Center. What are its goals in relation to low verbal deaf people?

Crossroads Rehabilitation Center, like other rehabilitation centers, accepted occasional deaf clients almost from the time it opened its doors 36 years ago. Our referrals mostly came from the Indiana School for the Deaf. But gradually, as more staff were added to meet the growing demands of clients, out-of-state clients were accepted. In a sense, all of our clients could be considered multiply-handicapped with a combination of psychological or physical problems, mental, educational or cultural retardation. We have a large number of Black people. Although Crossroads now accepts all kinds of clients and there was no thought of orienting it more towards low verbal Black deaf people, it was agreed that the special problems of these people had gone unrecognized and unmet too long and that we should give more effort to meeting these needs.

As a result of the Crossroads program, Flanner House, a home for young deaf adults emerged. What was that?

The grant for Flanner House was terminated in 1977. We had a home living environment and a structured work program for young deaf men in order to teach them independent living skills. In essence, it was a halfway house, a vehicle we hoped would improve their self-concept and encourage them to do as much as possible for themselves. Our grant money with the Model Cities program ran out.

What do you see for yourself in the future?

I have worked for the P. R. Mallory Electronics Company for 31 years. I have been thinking of continuing my schooling and working with the deaf in a counseling capacity.

Charles Williams

Charles (Chuck) Williams was born in Cleveland, Ohio, in 1931. He is chairman of the Black Deaf Caucus. Chuck attended California State University at Northridge, participating in Project DAWN, and also Cuyahoga Community College in Cleveland. He is currently on the Ohio Governor's Committee for Employment of the Handicapped and works throughout Ohio for better rehabilitation services and quality interpreting services for deaf people.

Chuck has worked extensively in workshops ranging from education to grant writing. He brought suit against the 1980 Republican and Democratic Conventions for their failure to provide interpreters for the deaf television viewers. We began our interview by inquiring about his early education and family experiences.

Charles, what were your early educational experiences like?

Until the sixth grade, my school day experiences were similar to those of other children. At the age of 12, though, a hearing loss was detected. This came as a surprise to the teacher, but was even more of a surprise to me. Although my older brother was deaf as a result of German measles, doctors could not explain my hearing loss other than to say it was nerve damage.

I was then faced with the decision of staying in the same public school or attending classes at the Alexander Graham Bell school. It seemed to me that my brother was enjoying himself on the playground as he and his friends talked with their hands, laughed, and ran about during recess. Understandably, I chose A. G. Bell.

Unfortunately, Ohio had been an extremely strict "oral" state; sign language was not permitted in the classroom. (I recall having my hands slapped many times as I began to adopt this new way of communication). While teachers may have believed they were doing the right thing by forcing us to attend lipreading and speech classes, we deaf children were really not being *educated*. The teachers were simply not qualified to teach children who happened to be deaf. I was dependent, then, on lipreading and whatever was written on the blackboard. I could not participate in classroom discussions, was "left out" of conversations, and began to feel that I was wasting my time. Those are the bitter memories for me.

Fondly, I remember my school days at the Ohio School for the Deaf in Columbus, Ohio. It was a disadvantage, though, to be starting there in the tenth grade. Sign language was still new to me. I was a frustrated lipreader, but gradually I learned to communicate with my hands as well. Not only could I communicate, but now I could also participate in things like the football team. Overall, I felt that more teaching and educating took place in a school where the focus was not primarily just on learning to pronounce words correctly.

We understand you also participated in project DAWN. How did that affect you?

In 1970, I was fortunate enough to be chosen as a DAWN participant. The *Deaf Adults With Needs* seminar took place at California State University at

Northridge (CSUN). Under the direction of a terrific man, Dr. Ray Jones, I learned how to deal with people, acquired skills in organization and development of programs for hearing-impaired persons, and learned about my own behavior. My respect for other people increased, as well as my tolerance and ability to share with others. Although I did not have a college education, Dr. Jones was willing to give me the chance to join DAWN; I am forever grateful to him. He is a hearing man who possesses knowledge of and, more importantly, feelings for deaf persons.

Another hearing man in Cleveland, Ohio, also encouraged "grass-roots" persons to use their talents. Mike Bailis was not afraid to learn about deafness and learn from deaf people. Thanks to his perserverance and sensitivity, he organized one of the first mental health classes to train deaf para-professionals. Approximately 12 hearing-impaired and deaf persons attended that course as well as a refresher English course at Cuyahoga Community College for almost two years. Mike Bailis is an openminded man who believed in treating hearing-impaired students the same way as any other CCC student. His course was strict and the field experiences were especially beneficial. While visiting institutions, we learned to deal better with people and respect differing opinions.

I have been very lucky to have had a close, loving family. As a young-ster who attended oral schools, my parents never believed in sign language. They, like so many other hearing parents, listened to the professionals who professed that oralism was best. Now they see that sign language truly belongs to deaf people and are even more supportive of my activities and the responsibilities I assume.

In view of your broad experience, what do you see in the future for Black deaf people?

I look forward to Black deaf people becoming more educated about political organizations and processes, more involved with voting procedures and rights, and more socially active. It is time to break out of the "ghetto areas" and "catch up" with today's society. More workshops need to be offered across the United States, older deaf adults need to get back into adult education programs, and break into the job market. Deaf persons are not only unemployed but usually underemployed. We must learn to keep pace with the changing times, learn to operate modernized equip-ment like the TDD's, and generally become stronger and independent.

Black deaf children are "better off" than during my days in school. Now they can attend almost any school, thanks to recent legislation like Public Law 94-142 and the Rehabilitation Act of 1973. We deaf adults must ensure that our children take advantage of these legislative changes and must insist that the courts and law-makers enforce what has been set down on paper.

Often, Black deaf adults are "set in their ways" and refuse to go into clubs comprised mainly of white deaf people. They often lack formal education and are resistant to change. We must encourage our children to reverse that pattern while still maintaining their dignity as Black deaf persons.

As chairman, what do you see as the role of the Black Deaf Caucus?

While workshops are not always a solution, the Black Deaf Caucus can begin to organize some, which will, first of all, educate Black deaf adults about their rights. We need to provide opportunities for them to get involved in politics, learn social skills, and acquire higher position jobs. We can establish leadership train-ing programs which will enable people to eventually have more control over their lives. Perhaps someday the Black Deaf Caucus will become strong enough to create an independent organization.

Are We Really Different?

Are we really different? One must understand that attitudes, like myths, are hard to get rid of and one's skin color and hair texture cannot be permanently changed. One must realize that from a historical perspective, race has and continues to be an issue when judging individuals. Aside from attitude and race, are we, deaf people, different from each other, collectively speaking? Let us take communication, for example, since it is one of the major handicaps facing persons with hearing impairments. Black deaf people (can or cannot) learn to lipread and speak as well as white deaf people can. Consider your response and rationale for choosing. Although we know that individual differences exist, even within a race, our reaction to issues and towards people depends on our attitude, experiences, and prejudices.

Most of us, Black and white, have some sort of racist attitudes and stereotyped ideas. Most are so deep-seated and buried that we are unaware of them unless challenged or forced to respond to certain situations or issues. From this framework let us view this chapter.

As pointed out in the beginning of this book, "the major problems faced by Black deaf people are undereducation and underemployment . . ." The same two descriptions are often used when characterizing the deaf population in general. Are Black deaf people really different? Except for being Black and suffering the trials and tribulations resulting from "too much" pigmentation, our deafness is no more difficult nor any less so than a white person's deafness. Another problem mentioned earlier was "an unfavorable self-image." This, we believe, is the REAL problem. This is where the real difference lies—in the measure of self-esteem. Poor self-image is more pronounced in young Black deaf persons. They lack role models and are often not aware of the increasing number of successful Black deaf adults until they are themselves adults and more or less set in their aspirations. Exceptions may be found in Chicago, New York, and the Washington metropolitan area. This general lack of awareness is not limited to Black kids. It is also widespread among parents and many career counselors.

Unlike most cities and many states, the Washington metropolitan area has a number of Black deaf professional persons in a variety of roles and a sizeable population of successful Black deaf, middle class families and individuals who are not college graduates. It also has its share of poor, undereducated, and unskilled Black deaf people, and street-wise deaf hustlers. Under close scrutiny, one would notice that the Black deaf middle class has more in common with their white deaf, middle class peers and acquaintances than with their street brothers.

While at a social gathering, we decided to have an impromptu interview with a friend who became hard-of-hearing during her late teens. We asked, "How does being Black and hard-of-hearing affect you socially, emotionally, or otherwise when compared to those years when you could hear?" She replied, "No difference. Doesn't affect me at all . . . no change. But if you ask me about being Black, I can tell you 'cause I know we live in a racist world."

This incident, again, shows that being deaf is the lesser issue and is not an overriding one at that. But being Black has major significance. Therefore, the problems of Black deaf people, if not different from deaf people in general, usually are race related or caused by race related issues, events, and attitudinal barriers.

When reading through law briefs or similar publications, one notices phrases like, ". . . lawsuit filed on behalf of Blacks, poor whites, and American Indians." Of the three groups, whites are qualified with the word "poor" while Blacks and American Indians are generalized. This illustrates the unconscious thinking of society, whereas in reality they know that culturally advantaged Blacks can and do hold their own with their white peers. We realize that poor Blacks are usually more disadvantaged than poor whites and that the Black middle class is not exactly the social equal of the white middle class, whether deaf or hearing.

Our attempt here is not at racial hairsplitting but to point out some of the dynamics inherent in being Black and deaf. Segregation within the deaf community is mainly due to the differences in educational, social, and cultural backgrounds, and in communication. Often segregation of the races among the deaf tends to be mutual, especially in cities where the deaf population is large. It provides a dilemma to those who would like to integrate. Two Washington, D.C., area clubs, MWAD (predominantly white) and CCAD (predominantly Black), are housed 12 blocks apart and are open to all races. Although members from each club intermingle, there is no great effort to integrate on a widespread scale.

Returning to the issue of self-image, it used to be that Black deaf persons of college calibre did not attend college due to one or more of the following reasons: Gallaudet College did not admit Blacks; they were unaware of the advantages of a college education beyond becoming a teacher of the deaf; they would rather work in a factory and "make more money"; or they were told that they were not capable of doing college work. Today, they have a variety of career choices and postsecondary programs to choose from. Some still do not choose to go to college. However, the reasons are different: "I attended college but I'm now drawing SSI;" "I have a family to support and I can't quit my job to go to college;" "A Bachelors degree is not enough, I will have to go on to get a Masters degree to get a good job;" "waste of time . . . ;" *ad infinitum*. These examples, which show a lack of ambition, misconceptions about college, and unawareness of the advantages of a college education, are not restricted to certain Black deaf persons but are also true of certain deaf persons of other races.

Jobwise, contrary to the general trend of high unemployment rates among Blacks, Black deaf people are usually employed and have a lower rate of unemployment than Blacks in general, although they are underemployed. However, this could change in the near future with the present practice of certain young deaf adults, fresh out of school or college or recently laid off, applying for and receiving SSI, "until I decide what I want to do." This will cause the unemployment rate to mushroom, Section 504 notwithstanding. We do not condemn this practice, in fact we are in favor of it because it does help those who are in need despite the abusers. An analogy to this would be the thousands of ineligible Blacks and whites drawing welfare benefits they should not get, yet who go undetected.

The average person's day includes one's work, family, society, and self. Deafness adds a fifth dimension. The type of work one does, the person one marries, the kind of friends one chooses, the way one sees himself, are all influenced by deafness and race, or influenced by either one of them to a marked degree at one time or another.

It is often said that no two people are alike and it has in fact virtually become a universal truth. It is also widely said that no two deaf people are alike—we are all different. However, by the same token we conclude that deafness has the same effect on a person despite racial, ethnic, or cultural background, but where Black deaf persons are concerned, the differentiating factor lies in being Black rather than in being deaf.

The Authors

Ernest E. Hairston

Ernest E. Hairston is an Education Program Specialist with the U.S. Department of Education's Office of Special Education and Rehabilitative Services. He is project officer for a variety of educational media and educational technology programs while, at the same time, studying for a doctoral degree in Special Educational Administration.

He holds a Master's degree in Educational Administration from California State University, Northridge. At CSUN, he was also a member of the National Leadership Training Program, Class of 1967. His Bachelor's degree is from Gallaudet College. Mr. Hairston has taught at the Governor Morehead School for the Deaf in Raleigh, North Carolina, and at the Michigan Association for Better Hearing and Speech; served as coordinator of the deaf program at the Michigan State Technical Institute and Rehabilitation Center; and was project director for Project DEAF at the Goodwill Industries Rehabilitation Center of Central Ohio.

Mr. Hairston received the George M. Teagarden award for creative poetry while a student at Gallaudet College. Since then, he has authored or co-authored a variety of articles ranging from "Educational Media for Mentally Retarded Children" to "Career Education for the Deaf in the Seventies" and from "Services to Black Deaf Persons" to "The Future: Hidden Captions, Videodisc, Micro-Computers, and Telecommunication."

Being active in organizations of and for the deaf, he has served in various official capacities with state and local associations of the deaf in Michigan, Ohio, and the Washington metropolitan area. He is on the boards or advisory councils of various community, professional, and educational organizations.

Ernie's other extracurricular activities include dancing-performing, karate, chess, computers, and rope jumping.

Linwood Smith

Linwood Smith is an Educational Specialist for deaf mentally ill and emotionally disturbed children and adults at Saint Elizabeths Hospital in Washington, D.C. He was formerly the Program Coordinator of the National Center for Law and the Deaf at Gallaudet College. Born in Lumberton, North Carolina, he became deaf at the age of two. He grew up in Washington, D.C., and received his B.A. degree from Gallaudet College in 1965. He obtained his M.A. degree from California State University at Northridge in 1971, where he was a member of the National Leadership Training Program in the area of deafness.

Mr. Smith has taught at the Governor Morehead School for the Deaf and Blind in Raleigh, North Carolina, and served as Guidance Counselor at the North Carolina School for the Deaf in Morganton, North Carolina.

An accomplished poet and writer, he has been published widely. His poems have appeared in *Symbolica, Uptown Beat, the Buff and Blue, Today's Negro Voices, the Gwendolyn Brooks Anthology*, and *Soul Journey*. He is also author of the book, *Silence, Love, and Kids I Know*. In 1965, while at Gallaudet, he received the George M. Teagarden award for creative poetry. Mr. Smith is the author or co-author of several articles on deafness, which include:

"Ethnic Minorities Amongst the Deaf Population." *Journal of Rehabilitation of the Deaf, Deafness Annual III*. 1973.

"Work-Study Programs and Black Deaf People." *Journal of Rehabilitation of the Deaf*. Vol. 6, No. 2, October 1972.

"The National Center for Law and the Deaf: An Open Door to Justice and New Horizons." *The Deaf American*. April 1976.

Also active in the deaf community, Mr. Smith has also served as president of the Capital City Association of the Deaf and the Washington chapter of the Gallaudet College Alumni Association. He is also on the Board of Directors of *Deafpride*, a Washington community organization working with parents of deaf children; the editorial board of *Mental Health in Deafness*, a professional publication for mental health and psychiatric workers with the deaf; and the Board of Directors of Otis House, the National Health Care Foundation of the Deaf.

Mr. Smith's interests are book collecting, pipe collecting, African art, and chess.

On November 14, 1982, Mr. Smith met an untimely death.

In Memoriam

It is not the critic who counts, not the man who points out how the strong
man stumbles, or where the doer of deeds could have done them better. The
credit belongs to the man who is actually marred by dust and sweat and blood;
who strives valiantly, who errs and comes short again and again; who knows
the great enthusiasms the great devotions and spends himself in a worthy
cause; who at the best, knows in the end the triumph of high achievement;
and who at worst, if he fails, at least fails while daring greatly, so that his
place shall never be with those cold and timid souls who know neither victory
nor defeat.

—Theodore Roosevelt

An enlarged copy of the above quote from Teddy Roosevelt was sent
to me by Linwood a few days after we had a difference of opinion over one of his
projects. On it was inscribed, "Have a good day! Your friend, Lin." These lines, in a
nutshell, indicate how he lived. He went about life in his own quiet way—oblivious
to critics and dissuaders. He enjoyed keeping many of us in a state of uncertainty
about his intentions or purposes and continued to do things HIS way.

The few of us who were able to penetrate his outer facade and gain
access to the inner person knew the real Linwood—a sensitive, caring, quiet, and
introspective person. He knew exactly what he wanted and where he wanted to go,
but gave the impression that he didn't. In the nearly 20 years I have known him, I
cannot recall Linwood speaking maliciously of anyone. He was a gentle person.
However, when something was not going his way, it was not beneath him to simply
get up and walk away or to divert his attention to something else without so much as
an "excuse me."

He was an artist in the truest sense of the word—a poet, a writer, and
a collector/seller of rare books. Nearly every wall of his home was covered floor to
ceiling with book-filled bookcases. In addition to this book, he was working on his
second book of poems at the time of his death.

Linwood, a dyed-in-the wool poet/writer, was just as happy among
his books, watching a captioned television program, or evaluating a movie for possible
captioning as he was at social gatherings—perhaps more so since he was an early
sleeper and early riser.

As much as he savored his solitary activities and preoccupations, he
gave of himself to the community by taking active roles in community organizations,
such as Black Deaf Advocates, Deafpride, Inc., and the National Health Care Foundation for the Deaf, among others. He gave as much of himself as he could spare and
apparently did not know how to say "No." He wanted to do so much, to please so
many in so little time. He was a strong believer and advocate for Black deaf individuals

and their advancement and was especially interested in deaf children and their education and mental health. As an educational therapist in the mental health program at St. Elizabeths Hospital, he was able to fulfill one of his goals. His poems, particularly the one entitled "The Way of a Hand," give evidence of his love and feelings for children.

Working with him on this book has been a fulfilling and rewarding experience. His absence is very pronounced since he was not only a friend, but like a brother.

May this book, an embodiment of one of his fervent dreams, serve as a fitting memorial to him.

"Whom the Gods love die young."—Lord Byron

Ernest E. Hairston

A Poem
THE WAY OF A HAND

There's beauty in the way a hand
   Can carve a word on air,
There's beauty in the way a hand
   Can give lift to a prayer.
There's beauty in the way a hand
   Can trace a song in space,
There's beauty in the way a hand
   Can light a deaf child's face.
Though, we can't hear the spoken word
   Or leaves rustling on a tree,
We can hear the beauty
   Of a word that we can see.

There's beauty in the way a hand
   Can make the things you say
Seem soft as rain, hard as stone,
   And clear and bright as day.
The spoken word can't do these things,
   But words in signs can be
More vivid and more meaningful,
   For they're something we can see.

There's beauty in a child's attempts
   To spell his first word "CAT,"
There's beauty in the way he learns
   To sign his first word "HAT,"
There's beauty in the way a hand
   Can move so gracefully
When someone signs "a stream of light,"
   Or "waves crashing on the sea."

Close your hands and cross them,
　　Draw them to your heart,
The word you sign is "LOVE"
　　And that's where signs should start.
Though, we can't hear the tinkle,
　　tinkle, tinkle of a bell,
We can hear the tinkle, tinkle,
　　tinkle when it's spelled.
Though, we can't hear the music
　　In the shells along the sea,
We can hear the music
　　Of a signed word's melody.

And being deaf we cannot hear
　　The baby when it cries,
Or the sharp loud crack of lightning
　　Sizzling down from darkening skies.

But we can hear the "cry and crack"
　　In all their majesty,
When they're clearly on the hand
　　And before our eyes to see.

　　　　　　　　　　　　—Linwood Smith

Bibliography

Alcocer, A. Editor, *Proceedings of the Working Conference on Minority Deaf.* Center on Deafness, California State University, Northridge. 1974.

Anderson, G. B. "Vocational Rehabilitation and the Black Deaf." *Journal of Rehabilitation of the Deaf.* Vol. 6, October 1972, pp. 126–129.

Anderson, G. B. and Bowe, F. G. "Racism Within the Deaf Community." *American Annals of the Deaf.* Vol. 117, No. 6, December 1972.

Austin, G. Editor, *Proceedings of the Utah Conference.* Professional Rehabilitation Workers With the Adult Deaf. July 1976.

Bowe, F. G. "Role of the Para-Professional in Inner City Services to Deaf Persons." *Journal of Rehabilitation of the Deaf.* Vol. 6, October 1972, pp. 120–124.

_____. "Nonwhite Deaf Persons: Educational, Psychological, and Occupational Considerations." *American Annals of the Deaf.* Vol. 116, No. 3, 1971, pp. 33–39.

Castle, W. E. "Education and the State Commissions." *The Deaf American.* June 1978.

Davis, A. *Social Class Influences Upon Learning.* Harvard University Press. 1965.

Ethnic Background in Relation to Other Characteristics of Hearing Impaired Students in the United States. Gallaudet College, Office of Demographic Studies, Washington, D.C. 1975.

Hairston, E. E. *Paradigm Of Identity.* Term Report, San Fernando Valley State College. 1967.

_____. "Overview on Problems of Black Deaf People." *Journal of Rehabilitation of the Deaf.* Vol. 6, October 1972.

Hairston, E. E. and Bachman, J. "A Study of a Segment of the Negro Deaf Population in the Los Angeles Area." Masters Thesis, San Fernando Valley State College. 1967.

Hairston, E. E. and Smith, L. D. "Ethnic Minorities Amongst the Deaf Population." *Journal of Rehabilitation of the Deaf: Deafness Annual III.* 1973.

Jackson, Jesse. "In Pursuit of Equity, Ethics, Excellence: A Call to Close the Gap." *New Directions.* Howard University. July 1978.

"The Negro American." *Daedalus. Journal of American Academy of Arts and Sciences.* Winter 1966.

Katz, L., Mathis, S., and Merrill, E. *The Deaf Child in the Public School.* Interstate Press, Indiana. 1974.

Kernan, Michael. "The World of the Deaf." *Washington Post.* February 26, 1978.

Lombardo, A. S. "An Examination of the Difficulties Encountered by the Black Deaf." *The Deaf American.* March 1976, pp. 23–26.

Lunde, A. S. and Bigman, S. K. *Occupational Conditions Among the Deaf.* Gallaudet College, Washington, D.C. 1959.

Magness, James. "The Main Problem of Black Deaf People: Education." *Journal of Rehabilitation of the Deaf.* Vol. 6, No. 2, October 1972.

Moores, Donald. *Educating the Deaf: Psychology, Principles, and Practices.* Houghton Mifflin, Boston. 1978.

Rowan, Carl. *Just Between Us Blacks.* Random House, New York. 1974.

Schein, J. D. and Delk, M. *The Deaf Population of the United States.* National Association of the Deaf, Silver Spring, Maryland. 1974.

Simpson, G. E. and Yinger, J. M. *Racial and Cultural Minorities.* Harper and Row, New York. 1965.

Smith, L. D. "Work-Study Programs and Black Deaf People." *Journal of Rehabilitation of the Deaf.* Vol. 6, No. 2, October 1972.

_____. "The Hard Core Negro Deaf Adult of Watts." *Journal of Rehabilitation of the Deaf.* July 1972.

Strassler, Barry. "The Black Deaf." *Dee Cee Eyes.* Metropolitan Washington Association of the Deaf, Hyattsville, Maryland. January 1973.

The Negro Family. Office of Policy Planning and Research, U.S. Department of Labor, Washington, D.C. 1965.

Vernon, McCay. "The Failure of Education of the Deaf." *The Buff and Blue.* Gallaudet College, Washington D.C. March 12, 1968.

Vernon, M. and Makowsky, B. "Deafness and Minority Group Dynamics." *The California News.* February 1970, pp. 3–16.

Vernon, M. and Mindel, E. *They Grow In Silence.* National Association of the Deaf, Silver Spring, Maryland. 1971.

Whitaker, Effie. "The Negro Deaf Adult in North Carolina." *American Annals of the Deaf.* Vol. 92, 1947.

Whiting, H. A. "Services to the Black Deaf Adult." Masters Thesis, University of Wisconsin. 1975.

Williams, Boyce. "National Trends in Rehabilitation Services to the Hearing Impaired." Paper delivered to the Oklahoma Council for the Hearing Impaired. Tulsa, Oklahoma. 1972.

Woodward, James. "Black Southern Signing." *Language in Society.* Vol. 5, No. 1, 1975, pp. 211–218.